Bergen for the Defense

By Marty Bergen

Bergen Books

Bergen Books
9 River Chase Terrace
Palm Beach Gardens, FL 33418-6817

First Edition published 2004.
Printed in the United States of America.
10 9 8 7 6 5 4 3 2 1

First Printing: September 2004

Library of Congress Control Number: 2004096304

ISBN: 0-9744714-3-7

Dedication

In Memory of
Alfred Sheinwold

In appreciation of his outstanding book,
"Five Weeks To Winning Bridge"
which got me started in this wonderful game.

Bridge Books by Marty Bergen

Declarer Play the Bergen Way

Bergen's Best Bridge Tips

Bergen's Best Bridge Quizzes, Vol. 1

To Open, or Not to Open

Better Rebidding with Bergen

Hand Evaluation: Points, Schmoints!

Understanding 1NT Forcing

Marty Sez

Marty Sez...Volume 2

Marty Sez...Volume 3

POINTS SCHMOINTS!

More POINTS SCHMOINTS!

Introduction to Negative Doubles

Negative Doubles

Better Bidding with Bergen, Volume I

Better Bidding with Bergen, Volume II

Thanks To:

Layout, cover design, and editing by
Hammond Graphics.

My very special thanks to: Cheryl Bergen, Trish and John L. Block, Ollie Burno, Jim Canty, Nancy Deal, Pete Filandro, Jim Garnher, Terry Gerber, Lynn and Steve Gerhard, Marilyn and Malcolm Jones, Steve Jones, Doris Katz, Danny Kleinman, Harriet and David Morris, Phyllis Nicholson, Helene Pittler, David Pollard, Sally and Dave Porter, Mark Raphaelson, Jesse Reisman, Carl Ritner, Mark Rosenholz, John Rudy, Maggie Sparrow, Tom Spector, Nancy Stamm, Merle Stetser, Bobby Stinebaugh, and Bob Varty.

The Official Encyclopedia of Bridge – Fifth Edition
by Henry and Dorthy Francis, Alan Truscott

FYI

On every deal:
South is declarer, North is dummy, and West is the opening leader, so East plays third-hand to trick one.

E-W (East-West) refers to the defenders **(your side). You** are sometimes East, and sometimes West.

Every bidding diagram begins with West.

West	*North*	*East*	*South*
—	—	—	2♡
All Pass			

The dashes are place holders, and in the example above, show that the auction did not begin with West, North, or East. The dealer was South.

The "—" does not indicate a "Pass."

Contents

Contents

Section 3: Defense with a Capital "D"

More Good Stuff

From the Author

Welcome to my first (but not last) book on defense. I've tried to make this book as helpful and instructive as possible, so every chapter is based on a practical topic. Of course, as with all my books, I hope that *Bergen for the Defense* also proves to be entertaining.

Before reading the deals and tips that follow, consider the following. Even if you usually play matchpoint duplicate, in this book you should concentrate on defeating the contract. Until the contract has been defeated, don't even think about extra undertricks. By the way, on most deals, even when you're playing matchpoints, you won't go wrong with this approach.

Because no two players have the exact same preferences, I varied the format a little from deal to deal. Some are presented in "test your defense" form, so you have an opportunity to find the solution on your own. I included questions on these to help you focus on the most relevant issues. Other deals are presented as they were actually played.

Of course, you're always welcome to test yourself by covering up partner's hand as well as declarer's cards, or to avoid all tests by reading on without answering the questions. The choice is yours.

On most deals, the auction appears. If no auction is given, the N-S bidding was straightforward, and East-West passed throughout.

I recommend that you check out the back of the book. Here you will find:

I. Bergenisms: Pages 169-190
These "tip highlights" provide many practical, carefully-worded statements that can prove invaluable to the reader in countless situations.

A. Defense (includes signals and leads)
B. Bidding and Declarer Play

This book focuses on defense, but on some deals, the discussion of bidding and/or declarer play provides helpful hints that are worth emphasizing.

II. Reader-Friendly Glossary Plus: Pages 191-202
Practical defense-related terms and advice will do a lot more than just allow you to "talk the talk." This section is sure to improve your knowledge and technique, as well as clarify uncertainties and popular misconceptions. Almost all terms are discussed in the book, but I also included a few that are important, or in some cases, amusing.

III. Appendix: Pages 203-210
Odd-Even Discards and Upside-Down Signals
Two popular alternatives to standard methods.

Best wishes,
Marty Bergen August 2004

Setting the Scene for This Book

Opening bids based on the Rule of 20.
Five-card majors.

1NT opening bid = 15-17 HCP.
2NT opening bid = 20-21 HCP.
Jacoby Transfers

2♣ opening bid is strong, artificial, and forcing.
Weak two-bids in diamonds, hearts, and spades.

Standard Blackwood (not RKC).

Responding to Partner's Opening Bid:

Natural raises of minors (no Inverted Minors).

1NT response to a major:
Whether you are or are not playing 1NT Forcing is not relevant in this book.

A response in a new suit at the two level:
Whether you are or are not playing 2/1 Game-Forcing is not relevant in this book.

Defense:

Opening Leads: A from AK, and 4th best.

Signals: Standard

Chapter 1

Getting Off on the Right Foot

Cheapest of Equals

The purpose of this important principle of defense is to **give information to your partner about your holding in a particular suit.** Take a look at this example. The card played to the trick is underlined.

North (Dummy)
9 6 3

West (You)
K 7 4 2

East (Partner)
J

South (Declarer)
A

What do *you* know about this suit? When South captured East's jack with the ace, **it is clear that East also has the queen.** Obviously, if South had the queen, he would have been delighted to win the trick with that card.

It is also true that East can't have the 10. If he had the 10 along with the queen and jack, he would have played the 10, the cheapest of these three equal cards.

The concept of "cheapest of equals" is not as easy as it may seem, so I'd like to offer some clarification.

Cheapest of Equals Guidelines

- Cheapest of equals only applies when a defender is playing third or fourth to the trick.
- It is used by third hand when competing for the trick, or by either third or fourth hand when winning the trick.
- It applies on tricks 1-11 in both suit contracts and notrump.

Here are four examples of third-hand play.
You are always East, and North is always the dummy.
For consistency, West will always be on lead, and will always lead the deuce. The contract does not matter.
The card played from dummy is underlined.

On each example, which card should you play?
Because some readers prefer to answer on their own, my answers can be found on the bottom of page 17.

1.

	North	
	9 6 3	
West		*You*
2		J 10 7

2.

	North	
	9 6 3	
West		*You*
2		J 10 8

3.

	North	
	Q 10 8 5	
West		*You*
2		K J 9 6

4.

	North	
	Q 6 4	
West		*You*
2		K 10 9 7

Answers

1. Play the ten.

2. Play the eight. Because dummy has the nine, your eight will do just as good a job as your higher cards of not allowing South to win the trick cheaply.

3. Play the nine, which is "equal" to your higher cards, based on North's honor cards.

4. Play the nine. You want to save your king to "kill" dummy's queen.

My Kingdom for a Signal

There are three basic defensive signals: attitude, count, and suit preference. No matter which signal you are giving, before discussing them, the following warnings must be noted:

1. Although some pairs have special agreements, these signals don't apply to the trump suit.

2. **The only time you can give a signal is when you are free to do so because you are not involved in competing for the trick.** If you need to play 3rd-hand high or cover an honor, that takes priority.

3. Try to make your signal as clear for partner as you possibly can.

4. **Never signal with a card that you might need later on.** It is better to risk misleading partner than to cost your side a trick.

5. All signals are useless unless your partner notices them AND can apply what he has observed. Don't waste a good signal on a sleepy partner.

By the way: The signals employed throughout this book are *standard* signals. If you would like to know more about some non-standard signals, take a look at the appendix.

For each signal, thorough explanations and examples will be provided in chapters 2-4.

Attitude signal (chapter 2)

This is the most familiar to all players because it is the first (and sometimes, the only) signal they are taught. When partner leads a suit, a high card encourages, while a low card discourages. This is also true when you are discarding, regardless of who led the suit.

Count signal (chapter 3)

When declarer leads a suit, a defender should give count to let his partner know whether he has an odd or even number of cards in that suit. **With an even number of cards, give count with the *highest* card you can afford. When you have an odd number of cards, begin with your *lowest* one.**

Because it's as simple as that, supplying information to your partner regarding your length in a suit should be the easiest signal to give. In practice, players with less experience have difficulty remembering to give count as opposed to attitude.

Of course, knowing how to proceed after partner gives you a count signal is *not* a no-brainer.
For starters, you had better watch partner's cards. After doing so, you must also be able to figure out the likely distribution of the suit, before deciding what to do next.

Suit-preference signal (chapter 4)

This is used when you want partner to lead a specific suit. A play of a high card strongly suggests that partner lead the higher-ranking of the remaining suits (never trumps). On the other hand, a low card would suggest that partner lead the lower-ranking suit.

Attitude signals and count signals can be made only after another player has led. However, in several situations, a defender can issue a suit-preference signal with the card he *leads*. The most common of these occurs when you are giving partner a ruff, or attempting to do so. You want to let partner know where your strength is, hopefully to find you and get a second ruff.

Suit-preference signals can also be used in the following situations:

- partner leads a suit in which dummy has a singleton and you have an opportunity to give a signal.

- you are knocking out declarer's last stopper to set up your suit in notrump, and you want to identify the suit in which you have an entry.

- other situations where the only logical meaning for your signal is suit-preference.

Chapter 2

Do You Have an Attitude Problem?

Accentuate the Negative

A common dilemma for a defender is: "Should I discard a high card in the suit that I want led, or a low one in the suit I don't?"

Although many players are used to encouraging in their strong suit, a better method is available, especially against notrump contracts. Marty Sez: **instead of accentuating the positive, discard the negative(s).** This allows you to hold on to all of your good suit, hoping to win as many tricks as you can. You can easily afford to discard in your weak suit. After all, why keep garbage?

It is essential for West to appreciate this concept on the following hand. You lead the ♠Q against 3NT.

Contract: 3NT
Lead: ♠Q

North
♠ 7 5 3
♡ K 3
◇ K Q 10 8 7 3
♣ K 8

West (You)
♠ Q J 10 9
♡ 6 5 2
◇ A 6 5
♣ 9 7 3

West	*North*	*East*	*South*
—	—	—	1NT
Pass	3NT	All Pass	

With dummy's long diamond suit staring you in the face, prospects for the defense appear to be bleak. On your spade lead, partner plays the ♠2 and South wins the king.

Before play continues, it is time for your *mandatory* trick-one counting of HCP. You have 7 and dummy has 11, a total of 18 HCP. Declarer has 15-17 HCP, which accounts for at least 33 HCP. Therefore, your partner has at most 7 HCP.

At trick two, declarer leads the ♢J.
You duck and East follows with the ♢4.

At trick three, declarer continues with the ♢9 and again you play low. There is no hope of isolating dummy's diamonds; one of those kings must be an entry (East can't have both missing aces with his maximum of 7 HCP). However, you desperately need to see a discard (or two) from partner.
He follows to the second diamond as South
wins the trick on the board.

At trick four, declarer leads a diamond from dummy and partner discards the ♡7. Declarer discards the ♠6 and you win the ♢A. The ♡7 appears to be a low card, because the 2, 3, 5 and 6 are all in view. The spotlight is now shining brightly on you.

Question: What do you lead at trick five?

East's ♠2 at trick one means that South has the ♠A. South has 9 tricks: 5 diamonds, 2 spades, and 2 more in the suit where his ace sits opposite dummy's king. Spades are not the answer, so the only hope is that East has a running suit and you can find him *now*.

It is possible that partner began with ♡A Q J 7 4 and has tried to encourage in that suit. But, knowing that **discards should be treated negatively,** you should lead a club. Once you do, happy days are here again.

East did the best he could by discarding his ♡7. Discarding a high club would make it obvious to lead clubs, but, signaling with the setting trick is absurd – a classic case of *winning the battle, but losing the war*.

Here is the entire deal:

North
♠ 7 5 3
♡ K 3
◇ K Q 10 8 7 3
♣ K 8

Contract: 3NT
Lead: ♠ Q

West (You)
♠ Q J 10 9
♡ 6 5 2
◇ A 6 5
♣ 9 7 3

East
♠ 8 4 2
♡ 10 9 8 7
◇ 4 2
♣ A Q J 10

South
♠ A K 6
♡ A Q J 4
◇ J 9
♣ 6 5 4 2

Like It or Not?

North
♠ K 10 5 3
♡ 7 6 5
◇ A Q 4
♣ K 5 4

Contract: 4♠
Lead: ♡A

East (You)
♠ Q J 9
♡ 8 2
◇ K 7 5 3 2
♣ Q 7 3

You are East, defending against South's 4♠ contract. Partner leads the ♡A (ace from A K), and dummy plays low. The question is: should you encourage partner to continue hearts by playing the eight, or should you discourage him by playing the two?

When this hand was played in one of my classes, East couldn't resist starting a high-low with the ♡8. West dutifully cashed the ♡K and continued with the ♡3. East ruffed, but that was the last trick for the defense.

East exited with the ♠Q, but declarer won the ace and drew trumps. Declarer then discarded North's club loser on the established ♡Q, and scored up 10 tricks.

Even if partner's lead promises the A K, don't always high-low with a doubleton. Encourage *only* if you *want* him to continue.

Contract: 4♠
Lead: ♡A

North
♠ K 10 5 3
♡ 7 6 5
♢ A Q 4
♣ K 5 4

West
♠ 4
♡ A K 10 3
♢ J 10 9 6
♣ J 9 8 6

East (You)
♠ Q J 9
♡ 8 2
♢ K 7 5 3 2
♣ Q 7 3

South
♠ A 8 7 6 2
♡ Q J 9 4
♢ 8
♣ A 10 2

I hope *you* would have played the ♡2 at trick one. **With your spade holding, you don't need a ruff.** Once you have signaled low to discourage, West will shift to the ♢J. With this defense, South's fourth heart will *not* set up, and he can't avoid a club loser along with the ♡A K and your trump trick.

Stop, Look, and Listen

Respect partner's signals. He knows more about his hand than you do.

On this deal, you are West, defending against 4♠.

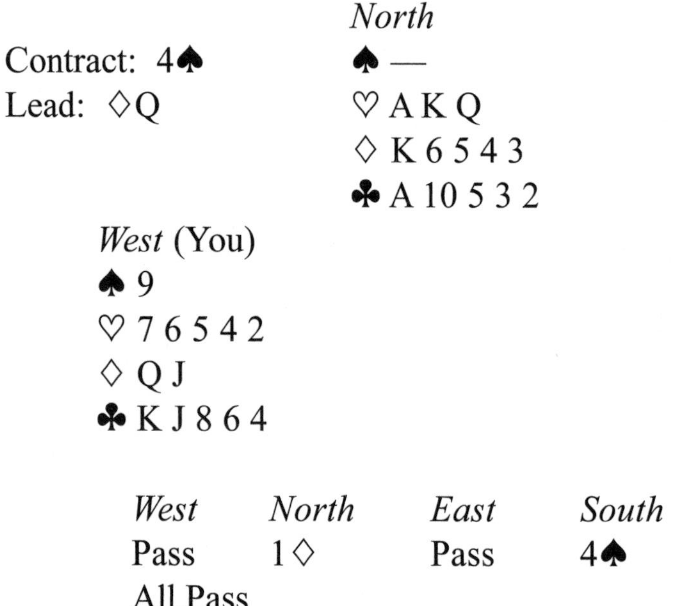

North
♠ —
♡ A K Q
◇ K 6 5 4 3
♣ A 10 5 3 2

Contract: 4♠
Lead: ◇Q

West (You)
♠ 9
♡ 7 6 5 4 2
◇ Q J
♣ K J 8 6 4

West	*North*	*East*	*South*
Pass	1◇	Pass	4♠
All Pass			

Despite North's opening diamond bid, you decide to lead the ◇Q. Dummy tables a nice-looking hand, although I have seen better trump support. On the first trick, dummy plays low, East plays the ◇2, and declarer follows with the ◇7.

What would you lead at trick 2? Make your decision before reading on.

Your opening lead worked out well. You are all set to continue with the ♢J, but pause to reflect on the seemingly contradictory evidence. What is going on?

On one hand, when your ♢Q won the first trick, you were quite confident that partner has the ♢A. On the other hand, when he played the ♢2 he was screaming, "I have no interest in diamonds." What in the world would cause him to feel that way? You would think that nothing could be better for a defender than to be sitting with an ace behind dummy's king *and* have his partner lead the queen.

Trusting your partner should always take priority over following your instincts. Why might he want you to shift? The only possible conclusion is that he has a void. Let's see, where could it be? He can hardly be void in hearts. You and North have a total of eight hearts, and it's hard to imagine South preempting with a 5-card major on the side.

However, you are looking at 10 clubs between your hand and dummy's. So, it's certainly possible that South started with three clubs. If so, partner is void.

You should respect partner's signal, and *not* lead another diamond. The correct defense is to shift to a club. How does this work out? Turn the page and take a look.

If you find the club shift, East will gratefully ruff, and his two trump winners will result in down one. If you lead anything else, South will discard his club losers on dummy's hearts and lose only one diamond trick and two trumps.

Here is the entire deal:

North
♠ —
♡ A K Q
◇ K 6 5 4 3
♣ A 10 5 3 2

Contract: 4♠
Lead: ◇Q

West (You)	*East*
♠ 9	♠ A K 4 2
♡ 7 6 5 4 2	♡ 10 9 8 3
◇ Q J	◇ A 10 9 8 2
♣ K J 8 6 4	♣ —

South
♠ Q J 10 8 7 6 5 3
♡ J
◇ 7
♣ Q 9 7

Chapter 3

Count Signals – Don't Play Without Them

You Can Give Count

Every player realizes the need to tell partner about his hand during the bidding, but communication between the defenders receives far less attention. This is unfortunate, because **defense is the most difficult part of the game.**

Every bridge player is familiar with attitude signals. A high card suggests to partner that he continue the suit. This encouraging signal is usually based on strength and requires good judgment. Attitude signals are given only when partner leads the suit, or when you are discarding. **When declarer leads a side suit, the appropriate signal to give is count**.

The good news is that signaling count is very easy. To give count, all you need to know is whether you have an even number or odd number of cards in the suit in question! And, would you believe, there is no bad news. You just need to get used to giving and receiving count signals.

Here's the scoop: when declarer leads a suit, (other than trumps), a defender who is not involved in competing for the trick should give count. The lone exception occurs when the information couldn't possibly be useful to partner and might help declarer. Because this is rare, **I believe in helping partner out by almost always giving count.**

How do you give count? Every player knows about signaling high-low with a doubleton. Two cards is an even number – as are four cards, six cards and eight. NOTE: if you have an 8-card suit but are on defense, we need to have a little chat.

With an even number of cards (usually 2 or 4), start with the *highest* card you are sure you can afford. When you have an odd number (usually 3 or 5 cards), begin with your *lowest* one. That's all there is to it!

How do you react to partner's signal? First, you must train yourself to notice his card! All the signals in the world are worthless if you don't pay attention.

These seven steps illustrate what you should do when declarer leads a suit and partner gives count:

1. Add dummy's number of cards to your own, and subtract that total from 13. The result is the total number of cards held by your partner and the declarer.

2. Notice partner's card.

3. Analyze partner's card and decide whether it is high or low. Twos and nines are obvious; middle cards such as fives and sixes are not. Sometimes, the other cards in view can clarify the situation. You'd like to know ASAP whether partner has an odd or even number of cards.

4. Consider the various possibilities of the number of cards partner has.

5. Think about how many cards are left for declarer.

6. Use bridge logic and clues from the auction to figure out the distribution of the concealed hands. Ignore any cases where your play doesn't matter.

7. Take the appropriate action.

Overwhelmed? Do not despair; a few examples will prove to be more helpful than any number of words.

Here's the first example. You are East.

	North	
	♡ K Q 10 5	
West		*East* (You)
♡ 2		♡ A 7 6 4 3
	South	
	♡ J	

South opens 1NT, which ends the auction. Declarer wins West's spade lead and leads the ♡J, and West follows with the ♡2. Let's zero in on the heart suit.

Step 1: You see nine hearts between your hand and North. 13 – 9 = 4, so you know that South and West have a total of four hearts.

Step 2: You notice partner's deuce.

{diagram repeated for convenience}

	North ♡ K Q 10 5	
West ♡ 2		*East* (You) ♡ A 7 6 4 3
	South ♡ J	

Steps 3-5: West's card is low, so he must have an odd number of cards; either one or three. Because South and West had a total of four cards, declarer must also have one or three.

Step 6: Declarer opened 1NT, so *he* can't have a singleton. Partner must hold the singleton, leaving declarer with exactly three hearts.

Step 7: You hold up your ace until the third round. Why is that? When declarer tries to set up dummy's suit, a cardinal principle for the defenders is: **wait until one opponent is playing his last card in the suit before taking your winner.**

With a different auction, you would not have known who had the singleton. Fortunately, there are often clues available from the bidding and/or early play.

For example, if the hand had been played in a suit contract, you would reason: if partner was the one with the singleton, he probably would have led it.

Now make a slight change from the previous layout:

	North	
	♡ K Q 10 5	
West		*East* (You)
♡ 9		♡ A 7 2
	South	
	♡ J	

Once again, South is in 1NT. He wins West's spade lead and leads the ♡J, and West follows with the ♡9.

Step 1: There are seven hearts between your hand and dummy's. The other two players have a total of six hearts.

Step 2: You notice partner's nine.

Steps 3-5: When partner signals with the nine, he has an even number of cards in the suit (if he has an unlikely singleton nine, your play does not matter). There are six hearts outstanding, so partner holds two or four, which leaves two or four cards for declarer.

Steps 6-7: If declarer began the hand with four cards, you can't prevent him from winning three tricks in the suit. Therefore, ignore that case and focus on the relevant one.

If declarer started with two hearts, you must take your ace on the second round; so duck the first heart, and win the second.

Although giving count can help your partnership in many situations, the most dramatic examples are the ones where the defenders have to decide when to release their stopper.

Here is a deal where giving and receiving count is crucial for the defense.

	North	
Contract: 3NT	♠ 4 3 2	
Lead: ♡K	♡ 7 3 2	
	♢ K Q 10 7 5	
	♣ 8 5	
West		*East*
♠ Q 10 7		♠ K 8 6 5
♡ K Q J 10		♡ 8 5 4
♢ A 4 3		♢ 9 8 2
♣ 9 7 6		♣ 4 3 2
	South	
	♠ A J 9	
	♡ A 9 6	
	♢ J 6	
	♣ A K Q J 10	

West	*North*	*East*	*South*
—	—	—	2NT
Pass	3NT	All Pass	

The bidding was short and sweet. With a balanced hand and the appropriate point count, you can't wait for stoppers in all suits to open 1NT or 2NT.

South held up his ♡A until the third round of the suit. Running five clubs tricks would serve only to help the defense count declarer's HCP, tricks, and distribution. Therefore, South immediately went to work setting up dummy's diamond suit.

South hoped that East-West would instinctively hold up their ace until the third time the suit was played. Having stolen two diamond tricks, South would then unleash his club surprise. He would have nine tricks; five clubs, two diamonds and the two major-suit aces.

Unfortunately for declarer, E-W were a good pair who relied on count rather than instinct. West could see eight diamonds between his hand and dummy's, so he knew that the other two players had a total of 5.

West ducked South's ♢J and observed partner's ♢2. West then knew that East had started with an odd number of diamonds. If East only had a singleton, South would have four diamonds, and no defense would prevent declarer from winning four diamond tricks. Therefore, West assumed that South had started with *two* diamonds.

When West was careful to win the second round of diamonds, declarer's goose was cooked, and he finished down one.

Notice what would have happened if South had held a third diamond instead of a fifth club.

	North	
Contract: 3NT	♠ 4 3 2	
Lead: ♡K	♡ 7 3 2	
	◇ K Q 10 7 5	
	♣ 8 5	
West		*East*
♠ Q 10 7		♠ K 8 6 5
♡ K Q J 10		♡ 8 5 4
◇ A 4 3		◇ 8 2
♣ 9 7 6		♣ 10 4 3 2
	South	
	♠ A J 9	
	♡ A 9 6	
	◇ J 9 6	
	♣ A K Q J	

West	*North*	*East*	*South*
—	—	—	2NT
Pass	3NT	All Pass	

All I did was exchange South's ♣10 for East's ◇9. It would now be fatal for West to grab the second diamond; South would still have a diamond to get to dummy. On this deal, East's first diamond play will be the ◇8. West will play his partner for a doubleton, and will hold up his ◇A until the third round.

If your partner hasn't been defending too well, could it be that *your* signals need some work?

Chapter 4

Suit-Preference Signals

Give Partner the Signal

Defensive signals are given after another player has led. However, because **suit preference is often given by a player's lead,** suit-preference signals are different from other defensive signals. It might even be helpful if they were sometimes thought of as *suit-preference leads*.

Suit-preference signals are ideal when partner gives you a ruff and you need to know what you should lead back. How can you find him so you can receive another ruff?

Observe the suit-preference signal in action:

	North
Contract: 4♠	♠ 10 8 6 4
Lead: ♢A	♡ Q J 10
	♢ K 8 4
	♣ K 5 2

West (You)
♠ 5 3
♡ 4
♢ J 9 7 6 5
♣ J 8 6 4 3

West	*North*	*East*	*South*
—	—	—	1♠
Pass	2♠	Pass	4♠
All Pass			

You lead the ♡4 and are delighted when your partner wins the ace. He returns a heart for you to ruff. The defense is off to a great start. Now what?

If partner has a minor-suit ace, you want to lead that suit. When he wins that ace, he can then give you a second ruff which will defeat the 4♠ contract. However, if you know what suit to return from the facts presented above, you are amazingly gifted.

The answer to the riddle, "Where, oh where, is my partner's ace?" can be found by examining the card he returned! Suppose that partner started with ♡A 9 7 3 2. After winning the ♡A, he has four cards available to lead back for you to trump (he hopes). The card he leads will tell you how to get back to him so he can give you another ruff.

Take a look at the actual deal. Because he has the ◇A, at trick 2, East will return the ♡9, his highest spot card. This tells you to lead back a diamond, the higher-ranking of the two side suits. If his ace had been in clubs, he would have led back the ♡2. In either case you will happily comply, delighted to receive the direction. If partner had neither ace, he'd lead back a neutral middle card.

Any partnership will be doing well if both players understand suit-preference signals. They can be used in a variety of situations.

Here is the entire deal:

	North	
Contract: 4♠	♠ 10 8 6 4	
Lead: ♡4	♡ Q J 10	
	◇ K 8 4	
	♣ K 5 2	
West (You)		*East*
♠ 5 3		♠ Q
♡ 4		♡ A 9 7 3 2
◇ J 9 7 6 5		◇ A 10 3 2
♣ J 8 6 4 3		♣ 10 9 7
	South	
	♠ A K J 9 7 2	
	♡ K 8 6 5	
	◇ Q	
	♣ A Q	

West	*North*	*East*	*South*
—	—	—	1♠
Pass	2♠	Pass	4♠
All Pass			

Trick 1: ♡4 lead won by East's ace.

Trick 2: ♡9 lead ruffed by West.

Trick 3: ◇6 lead won by East's ace.

Trick 4: ♡3 lead ruffed by West. Down 1.

Tell Me What You Like

North
♠ 9 5 4 2
♡ A Q J 5
◇ Q
♣ A K J 9

Contract: 4♠
Lead: ◇A

West (You)
♠ A Q 3
♡ 9
◇ A K J 3 2
♣ 8 6 5 4

West	*North*	*East*	*South*
1◇	Dbl	Pass	2♠
Pass	4♠	All Pass	

You are fortunate enough to have two very tempting opening leads. Although leading a singleton is very attractive when you have trump control, you choose to lead the ◇A. I agree.

The lead of the ace is more flexible. You retain the lead and will be able to take a look at dummy as well as see partner's signal. You then have the ability to lead whatever seems best. If you lead your singleton, you are no longer in control.

When dummy is tabled, you have mixed emotions. You're delighted that dummy doesn't have the ♠K. However, you're disappointed to see the singleton diamond, although not surprised after the takeout double and jump to game.

At trick 1, partner follows with the ♢4 and declarer plays the ♢5. It is now time to count your winners. You have three tricks: the ♢A and ♠A Q. All you need is one more. Before reading on, what would you lead at trick two?

Did you lead your ♡9, hoping that East had the ♡K or that you'd get a ruff? No offense, but I think you are being *very* optimistic! You and dummy started with 31 HCP, which leaves only 9 HCP for the other two players. For his invitational jump to 2♠, South needs the ♡K, and he probably has the ♣Q as well. No, I wouldn't suggest waiting for East to get in. If you think South will give you a ruff, good luck.

Did you think about partner's play at trick one? The ♢4 was his lowest diamond. What does it mean?

In a suit contract, when dummy has a singleton in the suit you led, if your partner is free to signal, it is not an attitude signal, it is suit-preference.

Because the defense would rarely want to lead dummy's void, that signal is very logical.

Aha! Now that you appreciate that East was signaling suit-preference, you know what to do. You should shift to clubs, the lower-ranking side suit. Declarer will win it on the board and lead a spade to his jack. You'll win and lead a second club. Partner will ruff and your ♠A will take the setting trick.

Here is the entire deal:

North
♠ 9 5 4 2
♡ A Q J 5
◇ Q
♣ A K J 9

Contract: 4♠
Lead: ◇A

West (You)
♠ A Q 3
♡ 9
◇ A K J 3 2
♣ 8 6 5 4

East
♠ 7 6
♡ 8 7 6 4 3 2
◇ 8 7 6 4
♣ 7

South
♠ K J 10 8
♡ K 10
◇ 10 9 5
♣ Q 10 3 2

West	*North*	*East*	*South*
1◇	Dbl	Pass	2♠
Pass	4♠	All Pass	

In Partner We Trust

Good defense involves trust. Consider the following:

Contract: 3NT
Lead: ♡Q

North
♠ A J 10 8
♡ 7 5
◇ Q 9 5
♣ K 9 3 2

East (You)
♠ K 6 2
♡ 6 4 3
◇ 10 7 4 3
♣ Q J 10

West	*North*	*East*	*South*
—	—	—	1NT
Pass	2♣	Pass	2◇
Pass	3NT	All Pass	

Declarer wins the ♡Q opening lead with his king. He then leads the ♠Q, losing to your king. You lead back the ♡6, which is won by your partner's ♡8. Partner then returns the ♡9 to declarer's ace.

Declarer now cashes dummy's three spade winners, forcing you to find a discard.

Question: What would you discard?
Make your decision before reading on.

Question: What would you discard?

Answer: Too many players rely on their instincts. They are reluctant to throw away a club honor, so they discard one of their "worthless" diamonds. Unfortunately, once they do, they have just handed South his contract!

Declarer will cash the queen, king and ace of diamonds and hope for the best. When your ♢10 falls under the ace, declarer's ♢6 will then become the ninth trick. Making 3NT.

Go back to trick three when West was left with the ♡J 10 9. He could have led any of those cards to knock out South's ace. Therefore, the card West chose to lead was a suit-preference signal.

When West led the ♡9 instead of the jack or ten, his suit-preference signal was saying that his entry was in the lower-ranking possible suit (clubs), rather than the higher-ranking possible suit (diamonds).

Because you were looking at all of the club honors other than the ace, you knew that partner had the ♣A. This entry was just what he needed to cash his two heart winners. Therefore, you can afford to discard a club, and South will take only three diamond tricks and will be down one.

Here is the entire deal:

North
♠ A J 10 8
♡ 7 5
♢ Q 9 5
♣ K 9 3 2

Contract: 3NT
Lead: ♡Q

West
♠ 7 5 4
♡ Q J 10 9 8
♢ J 8
♣ A 7 5

East (You)
♠ K 6 2
♡ 6 4 3
♢ 10 7 4 3
♣ Q J 10

South
♠ Q 9 3
♡ A K 2
♢ A K 6 2
♣ 8 6 4

West	*North*	*East*	*South*
—	—	—	1NT
Pass	2♣	Pass	2♢
Pass	3NT	All Pass	

Follow My Lead

This deal reinforces the principle of suit-preference signals when a defender is establishing his suit against a notrump contract:

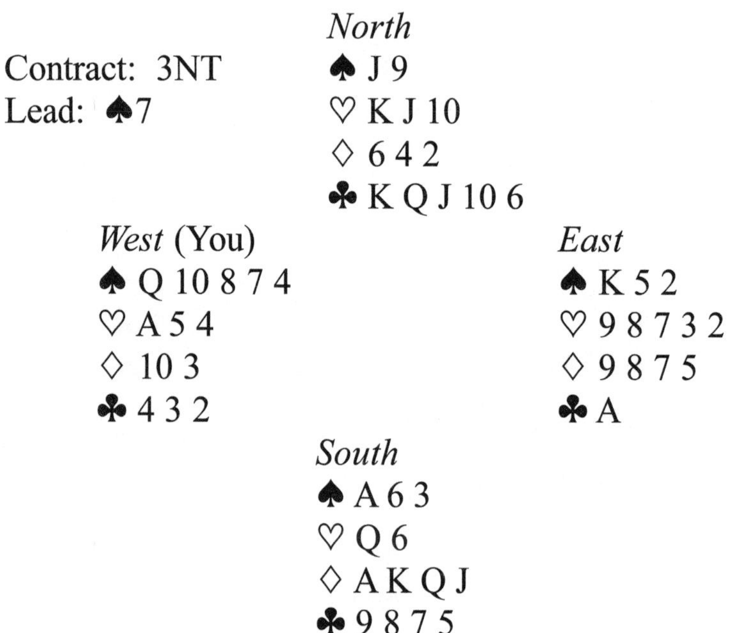

Trick 1: ♠7 to jack, king and 3.

Trick 2: ♠5 to 6, 10 and 9.

Trick 3: ♠Q (your highest spade) to South's ace.

East now knows that you have an entry in the highest-ranking suit. When East wins his ♣A, he'll return a heart, rather than *instinctively* leading dummy's weak diamond suit. You'll win your ♡A and cash two spades to defeat the contract.

Chapter 5

Applying The Rule of 11

Seven Come Eleven

Any time you think that your partner has made a 4th-best lead, you should apply the Rule of 11. Begin by subtracting the value of the card led from 11. The difference represents the number of higher cards in the other three hands (not including the defender who led the suit).

Do not lose sleep trying to figure out why this works; just accept it. The following *seven* points are also worth knowing about the Rule of 11:

1. It does not apply when an honor card is led. If you try subtracting a king from 11, all you'll get is an annoying headache!

2. Contrary to popular opinion, the Rule of 11 *does* apply in suit contracts – as long as the lead is 4th-best. If your partner opens 1♡ and eventually leads the ♡6 against a contract of 3♢, you can be confident that partner has exactly three hearts above the six.

   Because the opening lead in a suit contract will often be made in a short suit, you do need to proceed with caution.

3. The Rule of 11 applies on any 4th-best lead, not just on opening lead.

4. The Rule of 11 "works" any time a defender leads 4th-best. Of course, the lead of a high spot card usually reveals more about declarer's cards than the lead of a low card.

5. The Rule of 11 doesn't help the opening leader, but is invaluable for his partner.

6. If the Rule of 11 contradicts the cards in view, you can be sure that partner led top of nothing, rather than 4th-best.

7. Because partner would not lead 4th-best if he had a sequence, you can sometimes figure out who has a key honor. For example, suppose that partner leads the ♣7 against 3NT.

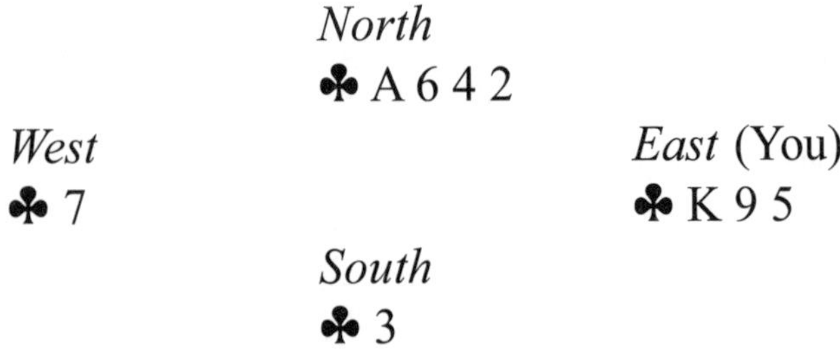

North plays low, and you win your king as South plays the ♣3. Should you lead back a club, or should you shift. Let's see. Subtracting 7 from 11 tells you that there were four clubs higher than the ♣7 between you, North, and South. You have two clubs above the ♣7, and North has one higher club.

Therefore, South started with only one club higher than the 7. Initially, you don't know whether he has the Q, J, 10, or 8 – but wait!

Can South have the Q? No way! That would leave West with ♣J 10 8 7, and he would have led the jack. You are now positive that West has the queen, so N-S have only one club stopper. Return the ♣9 and set up two additional tricks for partner.

Here's a chance for *you* to show your stuff.
As East, you are defending 3NT.

North
♠ 9 8 7
♡ A 4
◇ K Q J 10 7 2
♣ 8 7

Contract: 3NT
Lead: ♠6

East (You)
♠ K J 3
♡ 9 8 7 3 2
◇ A
♣ J 10 6 3

West	*North*	*East*	*South*
—	—	Pass	1NT
Pass	3NT	All Pass	

At trick 1, your ♠K loses to South's ace. South then leads the ◇3, West plays the 4, and you win North's ◇K with your ace. What do you lead at trick 3?

Did you make the obvious return of the ♠J? Tsk, tsk. South will then take the rest! The Rule of 11 should have told you that partner's spades were worthless.

11 – 6 = 5, so *if* West had led 4th-best, then North, South, and you would have a total of 5 cards above the 6-spot. However, North had 3 cards, you had 2, and South won the ace, which totals 6. This does not compute! The only possible conclusion is that West did not lead 4th-best, so he must have led top of nothing. Therefore, you shift to the ♣J. Before you know it, South is down one. Vive la différence!

Here is the entire deal:

Contract: 3NT
Lead: ♠6

North
♠ 9 8 7
♡ A 4
♢ K Q J 10 7 2
♣ 8 7

West
♠ 6 5 4 2
♡ 10 6
♢ 8 5 4
♣ A Q 4 2

East (You)
♠ K J 3
♡ 9 8 7 3 2
♢ A
♣ J 10 6 3

South
♠ A Q 10
♡ K Q J 5
♢ 9 6 3
♣ K 9 5

An Impressive Discard

Here's another opportunity for you to apply your Rule of 11 skills. You are sitting East.

North
♠ A Q J
♡ 9 6
◊ J 9 4 3
♣ K 7 5 4

Contract: 3NT
Lead: ♡5

East (You)
♠ 9 7 6
♡ Q J 8 2
◊ 10 5
♣ Q J 10 6

West	*North*	*East*	*South*
—	Pass	Pass	1NT
Pass	3NT	All Pass	

At trick one, you play the ♡J, cheapest of equals. South takes the trick with his ♡K and cashes the ace and king of diamonds. Partner follows to both rounds. When South continues with a third diamond, partner wins the ◊Q. The time has come for you to discard. Which card would you play?

Sometimes bridge hands yield absolute answers, and sometimes they do not. On this hand, there is only one correct discard.

Did you figure out that the answer is the ♡Q?

The Rule of 11 told you that South had only one heart above the five. At trick 1, there were six higher cards outstanding (11 – 5 = 6), and five of them were held by you and North. Therefore, declarer started with only *one* card above the five – the king, which he played at trick one. *You* know that all of partner's hearts are winners, so tell him loud and clear.

If you are wondering why this spectacular discard is necessary, take a look at the entire deal on the following page.

If you make any other discard, can you be sure that partner will lead a second heart?

From West's point of view, he would be afraid that declarer had started with a heart holding of K Q x. After trick one, the heart position would be:

	North	
	♡ 9	
West		*East* (You)
♡ A 10 7 4		♡ 8 2
	South	
	♡ Q 3	

If West leads a heart on this layout, he would be handing declarer an undeserved trick. Instead, he should attempt to find an entry to your hand, so that you could lead a heart through South.

Because of the Rule of 11, *you* know that West can run hearts. By discarding the ♡Q, you will make everything crystal clear to *him*.

Marty Sez: If your partner has not been leading what you hoped for – before criticizing him, perhaps you should take a look in the mirror.

Here is the entire deal:

	North	
Contract: 3NT Lead: ♡5	♠ A Q J ♡ 9 6 ♢ J 9 4 3 ♣ K 7 5 4	
West ♠ 8 5 4 2 ♡ A 10 7 5 4 ♢ Q 8 6 ♣ 9		*East* (You) ♠ 9 7 6 ♡ Q J 8 2 ♢ 10 5 ♣ Q J 10 6
	South ♠ K 10 3 ♡ K 3 ♢ A K 7 2 ♣ A 8 3 2	

Decisions, Decisions

Once again, you are East, defending 3NT. You're delighted when partner leads the ♠7, because you are holding ♠A J 9 2.

	North	
Contract: 3NT	♠ K 5 3	
Lead: ♠7	♡ Q J 9	
	♢ Q 3 2	
	♣ K 5 4 3	
		East (You)
		♠ A J 9 2
		♡ A 6 4 3
		♢ J 9 8
		♣ J 7

West	*North*	*East*	*South*
—	Pass	Pass	1NT
Pass	3NT	All Pass	

Here are the spades in view:

	North	
	♠ K 5 3	
West		*East* (You)
♠ 7		♠ A J 9 2

The ♠3 is played from dummy. Which card would you play? Stop and make your decision before reading on.

Your thinking should be: 11 – 7 = 4, which means that there are a total of four cards above the ♠7 between declarer, dummy, and you. You have three: the ace, jack and nine. Dummy has one higher card, the king. Therefore, declarer has no spade above the seven! Isn't that interesting?

It is easy for your side to win this trick, but your objective is to run spades. The ♠A is an absurd play; clearly, the opponents don't deserve to win their king. You could win the trick by playing the nine or jack, but what would you do for an encore? A spade continuation would allow dummy to win the king and limit your side to three spade tricks. It is difficult to imagine any other tricks for your side besides the ♡A.

If you believe that your partner is going to obtain the lead later in the hand, don't hold your breath. North has 11 HCP, you have 11, and your partner has the ♠Q, for a total of 24. Because declarer has at least 15 HCP, partner can't have more than a jack on the side, and all four jacks are in view!

The only correct play is the ♠2, allowing *partner* to win the first trick and retain the lead. So much for always playing third-hand high. This is just one of "a million" exceptions to that guideline. When West recovers from the shock of winning the trick with his ♠7, he will continue the suit. It will then be child's play for E-W to win four spade tricks plus the ♡A.

You should not be concerned that West might shift after seeing you play the deuce. West should reason: "If I just won the trick with my ♠7, my partner must have some great spades." Therefore, West will be thrilled to lead another spade through dummy's ♠K.

Here is the entire deal:

Contract: 3NT
Lead: ♠7

North
♠ K 5 3
♡ Q J 9
♢ Q 3 2
♣ K 5 4 3

West
♠ Q 10 8 7
♡ 5 2
♢ 7 6 4
♣ 10 8 6 2

East (You)
♠ A J 9 2
♡ A 6 4 3
♢ J 9 8
♣ J 7

South
♠ 6 4
♡ K 10 8 7
♢ A K 10 5
♣ A Q 9

West	*North*	*East*	*South*
—	Pass	Pass	1NT
Pass	3NT	All Pass	

Chapter 6

Notrump Opening Leads

Leading 2½ Card Sequences in Notrump

"Marty, have you lost your mind? How can you possibly have ½ card?"

Patience, dear readers. I obviously agree that I took some liberties with "2½ card sequences," but using this slang phrase is the most descriptive way I know of describing some non-obvious suits.

Let's begin with a quick review of some basics. **In a notrump contract, a sequence is defined as 3+ consecutive cards, including at least 1 honor.** Therefore, on opening lead against a notrump contract, lead the queen from Q J 10 2, but lead the 2 (4th-best) from Q J 5 2, because your suit is headed by only two consecutive cards.

When you lead the 2 from Q J 5 2, you will obviously not be happy if declarer or dummy wins your 2 with his 10. However, because you don't have anything worthwhile behind your Q J, there's a good chance that, even if you had led the queen, you'd be handing declarer a third trick in the suit. Qué sera, sera.

Marty Sez: even the best players in the world make some *very* imperfect opening leads.

Now suppose you hold Q J 9 8. Because you're missing the 10, you still don't fulfill the requirements of a sequence. On the other hand, this suit is a far cry from a suit like Q J 5 2.

I think of a suit such as Q J 9 8 as not as strong as Q J 10 2 (three consecutive cards), but much stronger than Q J 5 2 (two consecutive cards). Hence, I refer to it as 2½ consecutive cards.

Fair enough, you say, but so what? What difference does it make how you refer to this suit? But, it does matter. The bottom line: experts agree that, **even in notrump, it's correct to lead queen from Q J 9 8.**

They also agree that, on opening lead vs. notrump, lead the top card from each of the following suits, even though it lacks the third consecutive card.

K Q 10 9 J 10 8 7 10 9 7 6

When I teach this topic, I refer to these as a 2½ card *sequence*. Each suit is headed by two consecutive cards, with a gap of only 1 card before the next cards.

Of course, what you call these combinations is not important. All that matters is that they are *sequences*, and you should lead the top card.

That's my story, and I'm sticking to it. I'll conclude with a few frequently-asked questions on this topic.

Question 1: "Marty, all your examples of 2½ card sequences include two cards immediately below the gap. If I am leading from a suit headed by Q J 9, do I also need to have the 8?"

Answer: It's obviously nice to have as many useful spot cards as possible, but the additional one is not necessary. In reality, Q J 9 2 should be treated as a sequence, even though it is not as perfect as Q J 10 9. Because I'm a "glass half full" kind of guy, I do appreciate Q J 9 2 – much better than the usual Q 5 4 2 I get dealt. Therefore, regardless of what the "x" is, you should lead the:

king from K Q 10 x	queen from Q J 9 x
jack from J 10 8 x	ten from 10 9 7 x

Question 2: "Does anything change if you have a 5-card suit?"

Answer: No. Just as you should lead the queen from Q J 10 x x, also lead the queen from Q J 9 x x.

Question 3: "Why didn't you include holdings like 9 8 6 x and 8 7 5 x in your examples?"

Answer: Remember that a sequence must contain at least one honor, and the 10 is the lowest honor card. I would lead the highest card from these suits in a notrump contract, but now I'm leading top of nothing, as opposed to top of a sequence.

Wherefore Art Thou?

When your only hope is to "find partner," reject the suit(s) he has "denied."

Contract: 3NT
Lead: ♣5

North
♠ A 9 2
♡ A Q
♢ K Q J 10 6 5
♣ 9 6

West
♠ Q 7 5
♡ 9 7 5 2
♢ 8 4 3
♣ Q 7 5

East
♠ 10 6 4
♡ J 10
♢ A 9 7
♣ K J 8 4 3

South
♠ K J 8 3
♡ K 8 6 4 3
♢ 2
♣ A 10 2

West	*North*	*East*	*South*
—	1♢	Pass	1♡
Pass	3♢	Pass	3NT
All Pass			

It would have been futile for West to lead the unbid major (spades). If East had long spades, he could have overcalled 1♠. However, a club overcall would have required him to bid at the two level – not so easy. West led a club, and once the ♣A was knocked out, E-W were in control. When East got in with the ♢A, he cashed his remaining clubs. Down one!

The Dog Never Did Bark

"Bridge is a lot more than just a card game. It is a cerebral sport. Bridge teaches you logic, reasoning, quick thinking, patience, concentration, and partnership skills."

Martina Navratilova (tennis is not her only racket)

Here's another chance to see if you possess the same powers of deduction as Sherlock Holmes. You are West, playing rubber bridge. It won't be difficult for you to go quietly, because you are gazing at this *really* lousy hand:

♠ J 5 4 2 ♡ J 6 4 2 ◊ 5 3 ♣ 8 5 3

You	*North*	*East*	*South*
—	—	Pass	1NT
Pass	2♣	Pass	2♡
Pass	3NT	All Pass	

Obviously, your sides' chances of defeating 3NT are *very slim*. However, Sherlock and I believe that this opening lead decision is *not* an "eenie meenie minie mo" guessing game. Only one suit offers any realistic chance of finding partner. Are you with us?

Question: What suit would you lead?
Please make your decision before turning the page.

Question: What suit would you lead?

Answer: You certainly have no worthwhile suit, and it doesn't help that partner passed in first seat. Your only hope to defeat the contract is that partner has a long suit and you can immediately find him.

What have you learned from the auction? Declarer's 2♡ bid promised four hearts. Even if your partner has a nice heart suit, he is sitting *in front of* declarer's hearts, so your side is not getting rich in that suit.

The only reason for responder to bid Stayman is to locate a 4-4 major-suit fit. Since he did not raise opener's heart bid, he must have four spades. Obviously, the 1NT opener has two or three spades, which leaves partner with no more than three. No, the unbid major is definitely not the answer.

Many players progress this far and lead a club, because their clubs are longer and "stronger" than their diamonds. However, they're overlooking a very important clue. Sometimes your ears are more helpful than your eyes. In the famous Sherlock Holmes case, *Silver Blaze*, the key clue in unraveling the mystery was that the dog did *not* bark in the night. Who is that helpful canine in our story? It is your partner, of course.

With a very good club holding such as K Q J 4 2, A K 9 7 2, or even Q J 10 7 4, partner should have doubled the Stayman bid for a club lead. Once East did *not* double 2♣, your only chance to get lucky is with diamonds. Lead your ♢5 and hope that destiny smiles upon you.

For those who correctly figured out to lead a diamond, congratulations are in order. As you can see in the diagram below, your diamond lead will allow East to knock out South's ♢K. East must get in with the ♣A, and he'll run diamonds for down one

Here is the entire deal:

Contract: 3NT
Lead: ♢5

North
♠ K Q 7 3
♡ A 8
♢ J 6 4
♣ Q J 7 4

West (You)
♠ J 5 4 2
♡ J 6 4 2
♢ 5 3
♣ 8 5 3

East
♠ 9 8 6
♡ 10 5 3
♢ A Q 10 8 7
♣ A 9

South
♠ A 10
♡ K Q 9 7
♢ K 9 2
♣ K 10 6 2

A Lead to Avoid

Even in notrump, avoid an opening lead from a 4-card suit with the ace (but no king).

All of us were taught not to lead away from an ace on opening lead against a suit contract. Experience suggests that, with a 4-card suit, this advice should also apply in notrump. With this holding, you are more likely to give away a trick than you are to *develop* additional tricks.

Your RHO opens 1NT and your LHO jumps to 3NT. What would you lead?

♠9 8 7 ♡6 4 2 ♢A J 6 3 ♣Q 6 2
Lead the ♠9, top of nothing.

♠K 7 5 3 ♡A 7 5 3 ♢9 6 4 ♣6 2
Lead the ♠3. You prefer to try to establish your "aceless" suit. If you succeed in setting up spades, it will be nice to have the ♡A as an outside entry.

♠Q 4 ♡A 9 7 4 2 ♢J 9 ♣10 5 4 3
Lead the ♡4. With a 5-card suit, you have a better chance to develop a lot of tricks, and are less likely to give away a trick.

Logical exception: It is okay to lead from the ace in notrump when partner promised length in that suit. Leading partner's long suit is usually the best lead.

Chapter 7

The Right Time to Lead Trumps

Lead Trumps When You Are *Not* in Doubt

Everyone has heard the defensive maxim, "When in doubt, lead trump." Unfortunately, this is about as valuable as most other generalizations.

It is true that when you have unattractive holdings in all three side suits, you'll usually lead a trump.

Suppose you're on lead against 4♠ with this hand:

♠ 6 4 ♡ A J 9 3 ◇ A Q 10 5 ♣ K J 6

LHO	*Partner*	*RHO*	*You*
—	—	1♠	Dbl
2♠	Pass	4♠	All Pass

Your holdings in hearts, diamonds, and clubs are all screaming: "let *declarer* come to *you.*" The fact that, on this auction, partner has virtually nothing also suggests that leading a side suit rates to blow a trick. I'd like to think that every player would lead a trump.

Another reason to lead trump is when dummy has a short side suit. But how could you know that *before* seeing the dummy? It would be wonderful if you could take a peek at the dummy before leading. Of course, this is not the way bridge is played. However, on some hands, the bidding does enable a defender to make an *in-sight-ful* opening lead.

One example of a known short suit is an auction where the eventual dummy denied support for his partner's major-suit opening bid, such as:

1♠	1NT
2♢	Pass

Responder must have fewer than 3 cards (0, 1, or 2) in opener's major, so you can *almost see* dummy's short suit. Once you do, a trump lead is usually best.

Contract: 2♢
Lead: ???

North
♠ 6
♡ 8 6 4 3
♢ Q J 6
♣ A 10 9 7 4

West
♠ A J 10 8
♡ Q J 10 9
♢ 10 8 5
♣ Q 6

East
♠ K 4 3
♡ K 5
♢ 9 4 3
♣ K J 8 5 3

South
♠ Q 9 7 5 2
♡ A 7 2
♢ A K 7 2
♣ 2

West	*North*	*East*	*South*
—	—	—	1♠
Pass	1NT	Pass	2♢
All Pass			

When I use this deal in my classes, most Wests lead the top of their heart sequence without thinking twice. Unfortunately for E-W, after this lead, declarer should bring home eight tricks.

He wins the ♡A and concedes a spade. West wins and shifts to a trump, but it is too late. South wins the ◇Q and cashes the ♣A. He ruffs a club with the ◇7, ruffs a spade with the ◇6 and crossruffs clubs and spades with high trumps. Declarer ends up taking the ♡A and ♣A plus six trump tricks, and makes 2◇.

The defenders were poised to lead trumps when they saw dummy, but they had wasted their opportunity. Dummy's singleton spade should not be a surprise. In addition, West's imposing spade holding makes it clear that South needs to ruff his spade losers in dummy. West should ignore his attractive heart sequence and begin to shorten dummy's trumps.

After an opening trump lead, South has no chance. He will win and concede a spade, but West can then lead a *second* round of trumps. Once two trumps have been pulled from both of the North-South hands, the crossruff will fall one trick short.

If your opening leads are based solely on your hand, you're missing the boat. Your eyes will always provide a great deal of information, but for a bridge player, a well-tuned ear is essential.

The Thinking Man's Lead

West	*North*	*East*	*South*
—	—	1♠	Pass
2♠	Dbl	Rdbl	3♢
4♠	5♢	Dbl	All Pass

As West, you hold:

♠K Q J ♡J 9 7 5 4 ♢6 ♣J 6 4 3

Partner's redouble promises a nice hand, with some interest in game. Because you have no idea whether or not your jacks are worth anything, your jump to 4♠ is optimistic. However, you love your singleton diamond and three spade honors in partner's 5-card suit. When North sacrifices in 5♢, partner's double ends the lively auction. Time for an opening lead. What could be easier than the top of your spade sequence? Not so fast! Think about what is going on. Clearly, your side has the balance of power. What will declarer do for tricks? His only hopes are his trumps and short suits. So, lead a *trump.* In fact...

When the opponents sacrifice, almost always lead trump - even with a singleton.

You say that you were taught not to lead a singleton trump. That's good advice – in general. However, when the declaring side has limited strength, trump leads are the way to go.

Declarer won the trump lead in his hand and led a heart to dummy's king. East won the ♡A and led another trump. South won and led a heart to North's queen. He then ruffed a heart in his hand, which left him with one trump. Unfortunately (for North-South), declarer did not have a fast entry to the board to ruff dummy's last heart. When East got back in, he was able to lead a *third round* of trumps.

When the smoke cleared, 5♢ doubled was down four, a score of +800 for E-W. The ♠K lead would have allowed South to crossruff for down three, only +500. E-W pairs who bid game scored +620, so the extra under-trick was crucial.

Here is the entire deal:

Contract: 5♢Dbl
Lead: ♢6

North
♠ 6
♡ K Q 6 2
♢ A J 8 3 2
♣ K 9 8

West (You)
♠ K Q J
♡ J 9 7 5 4
♢ 6
♣ J 6 4 3

East
♠ A 10 8 7 3
♡ A 8
♢ 7 5 4
♣ A Q 10

South
♠ 9 5 4 2
♡ 10 3
♢ K Q 10 9
♣ 7 5 2

Time is on Our Side

When your side has strength in all the other suits, lead trump.

West	*North*	*East*	*South*
—	—	1♡	1♠
Dbl	2♠	Pass	4♠
All pass			

As West, you hold:

♠ 6 2 ♡ 5 4 ◇ Q J 10 8 5 ♣ A J 9 8

After your textbook Negative Double, your opponents arrive in game. What is your opening lead?

You're fortunate to have several attractive choices. You'd like to lead partner's major, but the ◇Q is also tempting. Which way should you go?

Both diamonds and hearts can wait. Your side has strength in all three side suits. If South has losers in a red suit, neither he nor dummy can have a strong suit that can be used to discard those losers.

Although you can't see the N-S cards, consider what is going on. The opponents can't have more than half the deck, so how did they justify bidding game? There can be only one answer. Distribution.

Your mission is clear. Lead trumps early and often.

North
♠ K Q 7
♡ J 7 6
◇ 9 7 6 4 3
♣ 6 3

Contract: 4♠
Lead: ♠2

West (You)
♠ 6 2
♡ 5 4
◇ Q J 10 8 5
♣ A J 9 8

East
♠ 8 4
♡ K Q 10 8 2
◇ A K 2
♣ 10 4 2

South
♠ A J 10 9 5 3
♡ A 9 3
◇ —
♣ K Q 7 5

South will win the trump lead in dummy, and lead a club to his king. You win the ♣A, and lead a second round of trumps. Declarer's goose is now cooked.

Because dummy has only one remaining trump, South can't ruff both of his club losers on the board. In addition to his two inevitable heart losers and the ♣A, he will eventually lose a second club trick and be down one.

On any other lead, declarer would have no problems. He would win the lead in his hand, and lead the ♣K. At that point, South can't be prevented from ruffing *both* of his small clubs on the board.

Tell Me More, Tell Me More

There are many auctions which scream for trump leads. So far, I have discussed auctions where:

1. dummy denied support for the major suit that declarer opened;

2. the opponents sacrifice;

3. your side has strength in all of the other suits.

Here are two more:

4. When your side opens 1NT, and you are on lead against a 2-suited auction, such as DONT or Cappelletti.

   The opponents are playing in a suit because at least one of them has shape. They want to ruff your high cards; you don't want them to.

5. When partner passes your takeout double of an opening bid of 1♣ or 1♢.

   Partner's "once every year and a half" pass of your one-level takeout double can only be based on a massive holding in opener's suit. Once you help partner remove the opponents' trumps, your strength in the other suits will allow your side to be in control.

Chapter 8

More Opening Leads

Look Before You Leap

Here's your opportunity to find the killing opening lead in the prestigious Spingold Championships.

Your underdog team trailed by 25 IMPs at the half, but both of your pairs had a solid third quarter. With 16 boards to go, your team trails by only 5 IMPs.

Tired but determined, you sit down to start the fourth quarter, willing to give it your best shot.

On the first board, you pick up a boring hand:

♠K 7 5 2 ♡J 9 7 ◇Q 10 7 ♣A Q 7

You do have four sevens; some would call that lucky. Perhaps it's a good omen.

The auction proves to be short, but definitely not routine. With neither side vulnerable, your RHO opens 5♣ and everyone passes.

It is time to make an opening lead. It seems like this is nothing more than a guess, but I strongly believe that the winning lead is totally logical.

Question: What would you lead?

Please make your decision before turning the page.

Question: What would you lead?

Answer: As you can see on the following page, in addition to your two obvious club tricks, your only hope to defeat the contract is to get your heart tricks. Otherwise, declarer will use dummy's top cards in spades and diamonds to throw off his two heart losers.

Those players who led a heart are undoubtedly feeling rather pleased with themselves. Should they take a bow? I think not!

Although a heart lead would have resulted in down two, a heart lead from ♡J 9 7 would have been my last choice!

When declarer has promised a very long trump suit, an attacking lead is the way to go. Clearly, leading from a jack is not an aggressive lead. Against this kind of auction, leading from a king is better than leading from a queen, and both are better than leading from a jack.

However, although a spade lead is more logical than a diamond or a heart, I'm not impressed by that either, and not because it would have been unsuccessful. I'm convinced that the only opening lead that makes sense is the ♣A. Your ♣Q 7 will remain as a trump winner, **but in the meantime, you get to see dummy, not to mention a signal from your partner.**

On this deal, after seeing the dummy and East's ♡8 signal, you'll confidently shift to hearts. On a different deal, with a different dummy, you might choose to shift to a spade or diamond at trick two. Regardless, by not prematurely putting all your eggs in one basket, you'll obviously have a better chance to do the right thing.

Marty Sez: He who guesses well is *sometimes* lucky. He who avoids guessing is *always* wise.

Here is the entire deal:

Contract: 5♣
Lead: ♣A

North
♠ A 9 8 6 4 3
♡ 10 4 3
◇ A K 9 6
♣ —

West (You)
♠ K 7 5 2
♡ J 9 7
◇ Q 10 7
♣ A Q 7

East
♠ Q J 10
♡ A K 8 6 2
◇ 8 5 4 3 2
♣ —

South
♠ —
♡ Q 5
◇ J
♣ K J 10 9 8 6 5 4 3 2

Making Something Out of Nothing

Although you'd prefer to lead from strength, sometimes you have no better opening lead than a "nothing" suit (a suit containing no honors).

To avoid trying to do too much, I'd like to restrict this discussion of "which card should you lead from a nothing suit?" to specifically xxx or xxxx, as opposed to longer suits with no honors.

Because this issue is less complicated in a notrump contract, I'll begin there.

Opening Leads from Small Cards in Notrump

Question: When making an opening lead from xxx or xxxx against a notrump contract, which card should you lead?

Answer:

- When the weak suit you are leading is one that partner never promised, **lead high** to deny strength. "Everyone" agrees with this. (Partner can promise a suit without bidding it by making a lead-directing double or with an artificial bid such as a Michaels Cue-Bid).

When partner tries to apply the Rule of 11, but it does not compute, he'll know that you didn't lead 4th-best.

- When leading partner's suit *after* you showed support**, lead high,** because he already knows that you don't have a doubleton.

Not all partnerships have discussed this situation, but virtually everyone would agree with the logic.

However, the third scenario would result in a more heated discussion. Not everyone would agree with either of the following, but here are my suggestions.

- When you are leading a suit that partner has promised, but you never supported:

  A. If partner is expected to have at least a 5-card suit, **lead low** to make it clear that you don't have a doubleton.

  B. If partner might have fewer than five cards in his suit, **lead high**. The logic is that if partner promised only a 4-card suit (or might have opened a 3-card minor suit), you would "never" lead that suit in notrump if all you had was a doubleton.

Keep in mind: Pages 90-93 deal with opening leads, as opposed to what to lead from a nothing suit at tricks 2-12. Once dummy appears, the outlook may have changed. **A different situation often calls for different strategy.**

Leading from Small Cards in a Suit Contract

Question: When you decide to make an opening lead from xxx or xxxx against a suit contract, which card should you lead?

Answer: There are three distinct schools of thought. In no particular order, they are:

1. Top of Nothing

Advantage	Partner will know that you do not have an honor.
Disadvantage	Partner will not know whether or not you have a doubleton.

2. MUD (middle, up, down)

Lead your middle card, then play the higher card to let partner know that you're not leading from a doubleton. The low card is played last.

Advantage	I apologize in advance to those who love MUD, but in my experience, there aren't any!
Disadvantage	It is difficult for partner to "read" your card at trick one.

3. Low

Advantage	Partner will know that you do not have a doubleton.
Disadvantage	Partner will not know whether or not you have an honor.

The choice is yours (along with your partner).

Question: What is the preference of the majority of bridge players?

Answer: From what I have observed, there is no clear answer. I suspect that supporters of school #3 are in the minority.

Question: "Marty, what is the expert point of view?"

Answer: Most experts, myself included, believe that, when leading weak suits in a suit contract, length is more important than strength. When making an opening lead in a suit contract, experts prefer to lead low from xxx or xxxx to make it clear that they don't have a doubleton. Most experts agree that those who use MUD will end up getting stuck in it.

Question: "Marty, do you ever lead high on opening lead in a suit contract from xxx or xxxx?"

Answer: Yes, there is one case. When I am leading partner's suit *after* I already showed support, I would **lead high,** because he knows from the auction that I don't have a doubleton.

Keep in mind: As always, all that should matter is that you and your partner are in agreement as to which card to lead in both notrump and suit contracts.

An Overrated Lead

Unless you're leading partner's suit, don't lead a doubleton without a good reason.

Why? Your short suit is often an opponent's long suit. Don't begin the deal by helping declarer develop what could easily be his key side suit.

Yes, a singleton is also a short suit, but it has a great advantage: once you lead it, you are immediately ready to ruff.

Too often, leading a doubleton doesn't work out well. The worst times to lead one are:

- When your doubleton contains one honor. Avoid 10x, Jx, Qx, Kx, or even the popular Ax.
- When you do not need a ruff, based on a trump holding such as J 10 9 x or Q J 10.

Obviously, you're always eager to lead a doubleton in partner's long suit (five or more). Here are some other good reasons to lead a doubleton.

- You have a sequence: A K, K Q, Q J, J 10, 10 9.
- The auction screamed for a lead of this suit (such as the opponents bid all the other ones).
- You have trump control (Axx, Ax or Kxx). Declarer can't immediately draw your trumps, so your chances of obtaining a ruff are good.

Chapter 9

Count Your Way to the Top

Know it All at Trick Three

Here is an example of confidently figuring out the distribution of the concealed hands.

Contract: 5♢
Lead: ♣A

North
♠ J 2
♡ K 10
♢ A J 7 5 3
♣ Q 8 4 2

West (You)
♠ 10 7 3
♡ J 8 6
♢ 9 8
♣ A K J 6 5

West	*North*	*East*	*South*
—	—	—	1♢
Pass	3♢*	Pass	5♢
All Pass			

*limit raise

You lead the ♣A, but declarer ruffs. He then draws two rounds of trumps. On the second round, partner discards a club. Add your two trumps to North's five and partner's one, which accounts for eight trumps. Therefore, South began the hand with five diamonds. Before turning the page, can you figure out declarer's distribution in the major suits?

Declarer was dealt five diamonds and no clubs, so he must have eight major-suit cards. If they're divided 5-3 or 6-2, South would have opened in his major suit. Therefore, his major-suit distribution must be 4-4.

Of course, once you know declarer's shape, figuring out partner's distribution is easy. You have three spades and dummy has two. When you add those five to declarer's four, you *know* that partner has four spades. Now you can do the same for hearts.

Here is the entire deal:

	North	
Contract: 5♢	♠ J 2	
Lead: ♣A	♡ K 10	
	♢ A J 7 5 3	
	♣ Q 8 4 2	
West (You)		*East*
♠ 10 7 3		♠ A 9 6 4
♡ J 8 6		♡ A 9 5 2
♢ 9 8		♢ 2
♣ A K J 6 5		♣ 10 9 7 3
	South	
	♠ K Q 8 5	
	♡ Q 7 4 3	
	♢ K Q 10 6 4	
	♣ —	

Unfortunately, on this hand, there's no hope for E-W. South will lose only two aces. Well bid, N-S.

Puzzle Solving

Here's another opportunity to practice counting distribution – one of the abilities that distinguishes bridge players from **BRIDGE PLAYERS.**

In class one day, two of my better students had the following auction (the opponents passed throughout):

North	*South*
—	1♢
1♡	1♠
2♢	2♡
3♢	Pass

Clubs were led and declarer (South) trumped the second round. At this point, it's possible to figure out declarer's exact distribution. When you're defending, this information is crucial. If you'd like to challenge yourself, take a moment to count declarer's hand.

Treat this as a puzzle. The first piece is that declarer has exactly one club. The next piece involves the spade suit. You can deal with it immediately because South's bidding has pinpointed his number of spades. Declarer did not open 1♠, so he does not have five. Because he bid the suit over North's 1♡ response, and never rebid spades, he must have exactly four.

{auction repeated for convenience}

North	*South*
—	1♢
1♡	1♠
2♢	2♡
3♢	Pass

That leaves South with eight cards in the red suits. You should tackle hearts next. Although some might think that opener has four hearts, this is not correct. If he did have four, he would have immediately raised the 1♡ response. Once he found a major-suit fit, he would not bother to look for a fit in another suit. Therefore, South has exactly three hearts.

Why would South support hearts with only three? North's 2♢ bid did not deny five hearts. North would need a 6-card heart suit to rebid the suit. Therefore, with a non-minimum hand, South should bid 2♡ here. Reminder: **opener would like to show his 3-card support for responder's major at some point.**

Now, and only now, can you count the diamond suit. With everything else in place, this is easy. You know that South has one club, four spades and three hearts, leaving him with five diamonds. The distribution of declarer's hand must be 4-3-5-1.

Because you can see dummy's cards, you know the distribution of three of the four players' hands. Counting partner's hand is just a matter of arithmetic.

The HCP Detective

As soon as dummy is tabled, each defender should add dummy's HCP to his own.

By keeping the auction in mind, you may be able to zero in on the remaining HCP. This is easiest to apply when declarer makes a very descriptive bid, such as opening 1NT.

	North	
Contract: 3NT	♠ J 3	
Lead: ♣J	♡ A 2	
	♢ Q 10 9 8 5 4	
	♣ K 6 2	
		East (You)
		♠ 10 8 7 5 4 2
		♡ K J 10 3
		♢ A 6
		♣ A

West	North	East	South
—	—	—	1NT
Pass	3NT	All Pass	

Dummy plays low, and you cleverly win the opening lead with your ♣A. It's time for a shift.

Question: What would you lead at trick 2?

Make your decision before turning the page.

Question: What would you lead at trick 2?

Answer: To begin, add your 12 HCP to the 10 HCP in dummy. Then add this 22 to Declarer's 15-17. Because the total is 37-39 HCP, partner must have started with 1-3 HCP. He led the ♣J, which leaves him with at most a queen.

If partner has the ♠Q, it does you no good. Your only hope is that he has the ♡Q, and that you can set up three heart tricks before your ♢A is knocked out. Lead the ♡3 (guaranteeing that the suit won't block), and hope that today is your lucky day.

Here is the entire deal:

Contract: 3NT
Lead: ♣J

North
♠ J 3
♡ A 2
♢ Q 10 9 8 5 4
♣ K 6 2

West
♠ 9 6
♡ Q 6
♢ 7 3 2
♣ J 10 9 8 7 3

East (You)
♠ 10 8 7 5 4 2
♡ K J 10 3
♢ A 6
♣ A

South
♠ A K Q
♡ 9 8 7 5 4
♢ K J
♣ Q 5 4

Counting to 13

Contract: 3NT
Lead: ♣3

North
♠ A 6 5 4 2
♡ J 10
◇ A J 7 5
♣ 9 8

West (You)
♠ K J 8 3
♡ A K
◇ 8 3
♣ J 7 5 3 2

West	*North*	*East*	*South*
—	—	—	1♡
Pass	1♠	Pass	2◇
Pass	3◇	Pass	3NT
All Pass			

You lead the ♣3 against 3NT. East tops dummy's ♣8 with the ten, and declarer wins the ace. He leads the ♡2, and you win the ♡K. Dummy's ♡10 and partner's ♡4 complete the trick. Once again, it's your lead.

You were not deceived by declarer's play of the ♣A. East can't have the ♣K or ♣Q; if he did, he would have played it at the first trick. Continuing clubs is futile; South will set up his hearts *long before* your clubs are good. What now? Count carefully. You know a lot about declarer's distribution.

Did you figure out that declarer *can't* have more than one spade? He showed five hearts and four diamonds and you can be sure that he started with the ♣A K Q. If he has a singleton spade, it could be any card, but as long as you're on your toes, it does not matter. Just in case his singleton is the queen, lead the ♠K!

When your ♠K drops declarer's ♠Q, the defense is in control. Declarer will probably hold up dummy's ♠A until the third round, but you're looking good with the ♡A and a spade winner.

Here is the entire deal:

	North	
Contract: 3NT	♠ A 6 5 4 2	
Lead: ♣3	♡ J 10	
	◇ A J 7 5	
	♣ 9 8	
West (You)		*East*
♠ K J 8 3		♠ 10 9 7
♡ A K		♡ 6 5 4 3
◇ 8 3		◇ Q 10 4
♣ J 7 5 3 2		♣ 10 6 4
	South	
	♠ Q	
	♡ Q 9 8 7 2	
	◇ K 9 6 2	
	♣ A K Q	

Chapter 10

Partnership Defense

You Be The Judge

The persons who feel it necessary to conclude each hand with a magisterial correction of their partners (and their opponents as well) have no place at the bridge table, or anywhere else they might come into contact with civilized beings.

Elmer Davis, bridge writer, Harper's Magazine

A bridge partnership consists of two individuals, who often have different points of view. Post-mortems are rarely dull, especially after a disaster has occurred. Rationalizing, partner-bashing, and damage control are inevitable, even when the participants are otherwise fair-minded.

For many years, the most respected bridge publication has been *The Bridge World.* One of its most popular features is "You Be The Judge" (YBTJ). A panel of experts examines deals played by other experts to decide where they went wrong. The analysis often becomes quite spirited as the panelists enthusiastically criticize their peers. In addition, the panel members also express their feelings as to which action was the most serious offense.

East-West put up an unsuccessful defense on the following deal. After observing the facts and hearing the post-mortem, I would like you to play YBTJ.

Picture yourself as the bridge teacher (judge) confronted by an unhappy pair of students (lawyers). I will conclude with my Supreme Court ruling – one advantage of being the author.

Contract: 4♡
Lead: ♠3

North
♠ 9 7
♡ A 10 9
◊ A 5 4
♣ A J 10 9 2

West
♠ 10 8 6 3 2
♡ 6 3
◊ Q 8 7
♣ 8 5 3

East
♠ K J 5 4
♡ K 5
◊ K 10 9 6
♣ K 7 6

South
♠ A Q
♡ Q J 8 7 4 2
◊ J 3 2
♣ Q 4

West	*North*	*East*	*South*
—	1♣	Pass	1♡
Pass	2♡	Pass	4♡
All Pass			

Notice North's sensible raise to 2♡ with only 3-card support for hearts. The three aces, heart intermediates, and worthless doubleton all strongly suggest that North will have a useful dummy in a heart contract.

West led the ♠3, and declarer captured East's king with his ace. At trick two, South finessed the ♡Q, which lost to East's king. East placed the ♠Q with his partner and dutifully returned a low spade. He expected West to shift to a diamond, and East would then win the ◇K and ♣K for down one.

South emerged with an overtrick. He won East's spade return with the queen and drew trumps. The losing club finesse was now totally painless, because declarer could discard his diamond losers on the established club suit.

What follows is East-West's animated post-mortem: "W" stands for West, "E" for East, and "S" for South.

1-E: "Why did you lead your weaker suit? If you had led a diamond, they would go down."

2-W: "How could I know that? If you wanted a diamond lead, why didn't you bid the suit?"

3-E: "I only had four diamonds. An overcall promises a 5-card suit."

4-W: "Not always! Haven't you read Marty's *Points Schmoints* book?"

5-E: "Of course I have! But Marty says you should have at least three honors for an overcall in a 4-card suit. In fact, his example features a suit of A K Q 10. That's a far cry from K 10 9 6."

6-W: "You could have shifted to a diamond after winning the ♡K. Then we'd have defeated the contract despite my imperfect lead."

7-E: "I know. However, if you had the ♠Q instead of the ◇Q, my defense was correct. Had I known you were a devotee of garbage leads, I might have figured that out."

7-E: "After your stupid spade lead, South was cold if he played clubs first. How could I find the winning defense when you misled me with your lead and declarer misplayed as well?"

8-S: "Hey, leave me out of this. I played the hand correctly. It was normal to draw trumps first."

That was quite a post-mortem. If E-W had devoted as much energy to defending the hand as they did to defending themselves, they would have easily defeated the contract.

Have you completed your YBTJ analysis?
Now it's my turn.

1. West *might* have preferred the more aggressive diamond lead.

2. An opening diamond lead was far from obvious.

3. An overcall usually promises at least five cards.

4. Yes, a one-level overcall can be made on a very strong 4-card suit.

5. You should have *three* honors in the suit when you overcall with only four cards. I would not have bid 1♢. East has a very flexible hand, with honors in all suits. He has no reason to direct partner's attention toward any specific suit.

6. Yes, as long as E-W were careful, a shift to the ♢10 would have defeated the contract.

{deal repeated for convenience}

Contract: 4♡
Lead: ♠3

North
♠ 9 7
♡ A 10 9
♢ A 5 4
♣ A J 10 9 2

West
♠ 10 8 6 3 2
♡ 6 3
♢ Q 8 7
♣ 8 5 3

East
♠ K J 5 4
♡ K 5
♢ K 10 9 6
♣ K 7 6

South
♠ A Q
♡ Q J 8 7 4 2
♢ J 3 2
♣ Q 4

7. East is correct: A spade continuation would be necessary if West's queens were reversed. Yes, South would have made the hand if he had played clubs first. Although the club finesse would lose, declarer would discard a diamond loser on the third round of clubs.

8. South's actual line of play was normal and correct. The only reason to play clubs at trick two would be if they split 3-3, *and* both finesses were destined to fail, *and* E-W had known to shift to diamonds. This certainly goes against the odds.

What gets my vote for the worst transgression? Would you believe it didn't even get mentioned? At trick one, East should have played the ♠J instead of the king. There's no risk because South is marked with the ace; **partner would never underlead an ace at trick one against a suit contract.** If declarer had the A Q, he deserved to win two tricks.

The play of the jack from K J against suit contracts is an example of a *discovery play*. It will enable East to discover immediately who has the queen (if declarer wins the ace, West must have the queen).

Observe how this play simplifies matters for the defense. Once East learns that the defense has no spade tricks available, the menacing club suit makes it clear that a diamond shift is necessary. After East leads the ♢10, the defense is in control.

{deal repeated for convenience}

Contract: 4♡
Lead: ♠3

North
♠ 9 7
♡ A 10 9
◇ A 5 4
♣ A J 10 9 2

West
♠ 10 8 6 3 2
♡ 6 3
◇ Q 8 7
♣ 8 5 3

East
♠ K J 5 4
♡ K 5
◇ K 10 9 6
♣ K 7 6

South
♠ A Q
♡ Q J 8 7 4 2
◇ J 3 2
♣ Q 4

In conclusion:

1. Use your energy for thinking during the play, rather than rationalizing in the post-mortem.

2. When third-hand in a suit contract, remember the play of the jack from K J at trick one.

3. Turn the page and read "21 Rules of Being a Good Partner," especially numbers 1, 3, 4, 12, and 13.

21 Rules of Being a Good Partner

I have always believed that your attitude toward your partner is as important as your technical skill at the game.

Rixi Markus, one of the all-time great players

Before you sit down to discuss what you are playing, you should start your partnership off on the right note. Half the battle of winning is being a good partner. Always observe the following guidelines:

1. Do not give lessons, unless you are being paid to do so. *According to an evening paper, there are only five real authorities on bridge in this country. Odd how often one gets one of them as a partner.* Punch (British magazine)

2. Never say anything to your partner unless you would want him to say the same to you. If you are unsure whether your partner would want you to say something, don't.

3. Never "result" (criticize your partner for a normal action just because it did not work this time).

4. Unless you positively can't wait, avoid discussing the hand just played until later. When you do go over it, be discreet.

5. Remember that you and your partner are on the same side.

6. Don't forget that your partner wants to win as much as you do.

7. If you feel the urge to be nasty, sarcastic, critical, or loud – excuse yourself and take a walk.

8. When you do have time between hands, *do not* discuss bridge.

9. When you want to consult another player about a disaster, ask about your hand, not your partner's.

10. Never criticize or embarrass your partner in front of others.

11. Remember that bridge is only a card game.

12. Have a good time. *Bridge is for fun. You should play the game for no other reason. You should not play bridge to make money, to show how smart you are, or to show how stupid your partner is . . . or to prove any of the several hundred other things bridge players are so often trying to prove.* bridge legend Charles Goren

13. Trust your partner; do not assume that he has made a mistake.

14. Although it may be unfashionable, it really is okay to be pleasant to a partner with whom you also happen to live.

15. Think twice before verbally analyzing a hand. Do not embarrass yourself with a hasty, inaccurate, or inappropriate comment.

    Remember: *The worst analysts and the biggest talkers are often one and the same.*
    bridge columnist Frank Stewart

16. When you voluntarily choose to play bridge with someone, it is not fair to get upset when partner does not play any better than usual.

17. Never side with an opponent against your partner. If you cannot support your partner, say nothing.

18. If you think you are too good for a partner and do not enjoy playing bridge with him, do everyone a favor and play with someone else. That is clearly much better than being a martyr. However, be careful before burning bridges – another player's grass may not be greener.

19. Learn your partner's style, regardless of how you feel about it. Do not expect your partner to bid exactly as you would. When partner makes a bid, consider what he will have, not what you would.

20. Don't throw tricky bids at partner. Seek the bid or play that will make his life easier.

21. Sympathize with partner if he makes a mistake. Let your partner know that you like him, and always root for him 100%.

Chapter 11

Entry Killing

The Right Time for a Merrimac Coup

Contract: 3NT
Lead: ♠10

North
♠ 6 5 3
♡ A 9
◇ 10 4
♣ K Q 7 4 3 2

East (You)
♠ A 7
♡ K 10 8 7
◇ J 9 8 6
♣ A 6 5

West	*North*	*East*	*South*
—	—	—	1NT
Pass	3NT	All Pass	

You win partner's opening ♠10 lead with your ace as South drops the jack. You're playing standard leads, so West's spades can be headed by either the 10 9 8, K 10 9, or Q 10 9.

It's time to count HCP. Your 12 plus dummy's 9 HCP totals 21. When you add that to declarer's 15-17, you arrive at a total of 36-38. Therefore, your partner started with 2-4 HCP.

What you would lead at trick two? Do give it some thought before turning the page.

Begin by considering the spade suit. It appears that South was dealt either Q J doubleton, K J doubleton, or K Q J. If he has Q J doubleton, he's going down. Your side would be entitled to 5 spades and 2 aces.

If South was dealt the ♠K J, he has only one stopper. You could lead your ♠7 and drive out South's king, **but West will never get in.** You and North have 21 HCP, and South has 15-17. If West has the ♠Q, he has at most 2 HCP in the other suits. Of course, if South had the ♠K Q J, leading a spade is also futile.

How formidable is dummy's club suit? Although North's spot cards are not very good, you know that North's club suit will be good for 5 tricks once South knocks out your ace. You and dummy have 9 clubs, which leaves a total of 4 clubs for South and West. South's 1NT opening bid guarantees at least 2 clubs. Even if your partner has the ♣J 10, they'll fall under the K Q, and dummy's ♣7 will be good.

The thinking above is all well and good, but it is not the bottom line. The key is: North has a long strong suit, but only one outside entry. If you can knock out the ♡A, North's long suit will no longer be a threat. Therefore, **it must be correct to lead a heart at trick two.** One question remains – which heart should you lead? Because of dummy's ♡9, the surrounding play of leading the ♡10 would often be the correct card to lead with this suit combination. However, if South plays the ♡Q, dummy's ♡A will remain intact.

This is no time for halfway measures. You need to remove dummy's ♡A, and there is only one sure way to do it. Don't send a peasant when his majesty is available. The only winning defense is to sacrifice your ♡K! For those who like colorful names, this entry-killing play is referred to as a Merrimac Coup.

If declarer ducks the ♡K, you'll lead a second heart. When South plays clubs and partner follows twice, you'll confidently win the second round. Although declarer has a 17-count, he will be limited to three hearts, two spades, two diamonds, and only *one* club trick. Down one!

Here is the entire deal:

	North	
Contract: 3NT Lead: ♠10	♠ 6 5 3 ♡ A 9 ◇ 10 4 ♣ K Q 7 4 3 2	
West ♠ 10 9 8 4 2 ♡ 6 5 3 ◇ Q 7 2 ♣ 9 8		*East* (You) ♠ A 7 ♡ K 10 8 7 ◇ J 9 8 6 ♣ A 6 5
	South ♠ K Q J ♡ Q J 4 2 ◇ A K 5 3 ♣ J 10	

When the Time is Right

	North
Contract: 3NT	♠ Q 8 7
Lead: ♡Q	♡ K 5 3
	◊ J 5 4 2
	♣ Q J 10

West (You)
♠ A 3 2
♡ Q J 10 9
◊ 9 7 6
♣ A 4 3

West	*North*	*East*	*South*
—	Pass	Pass	1NT
Pass	2NT	Pass	3NT
All Pass			

With your lovely heart sequence and two sure entries, you are delighted to lead the ♡Q. In fact, if you had a fifth heart, doubling 3NT would be clear-cut.

Your ♡Q wins the first trick, as partner contributes the ♡6 and declarer plays the ♡4. **After leading the top of a sequence, it is normal to continue with the bottom of the sequence,** so you lead the ♡9. Partner follows with the ♡2, and South wins his ace.

Declarer then turns his attention to diamonds by cashing the ace, king, and queen at tricks 3-5. Your partner follows to all three rounds.

Declarer leads the ♣5 from his hand. You're in no hurry, so you play low. South calls for dummy's ♣10, which wins the trick as East plays the ♣2.

At trick 7, declarer cashes dummy's ♢J. East discards the ♠4, and declarer discards the ♠6. Before making your discard, stop and think. It is possible for you to figure out *a great deal* about the hand.

Here are the important clues:

1. After opening 1NT, declarer has shown up with the ♡A and ♢A K Q.

2. When a club was led to dummy's ♣10, partner followed with the two.

Trust me, that's all that matters.

Question 1: What will you discard?

Question 2: If you defend correctly, will declarer make this hand – yes, no or maybe?

While question # 2 may seem presumptuous on my part, if you process *all* of the available information, a confident answer is possible.

Question 1: What will you discard?

Answer: You should discard a low spade.
You *must* hold on to your precious ♣4!

Why? I promise to tell you, but stay with me for a moment. First, I have another question. South now leads dummy's ♣J. Both East and South play low.

Bonus Question: Are you ready to win your ♣A?

Answer: No way! You must wait until the third club is played to release your stopper. **That is why you couldn't afford to discard a club earlier.**

Take a look at the actual deal on the following page. Once South played off his four red-suit winners, **he no longer had an outside entry to his hand.** Count his HCP. His ♡A and ◇A K Q mark him with 13 HCP in the red suits. When East didn't win the first round of clubs, South was marked with the ♣K. That brings him to 16 HCP. If he also had the ♠K, he'd have 19 HCP, and would not have opened 1NT.

As long as you hold up your ♣A to the third round, South can't get to his fourth club. Whether he plays a third round of clubs or switches to spades, he can no longer make the hand. In addition to the ♣A and ♠A K, your side will be able to win two heart tricks. The answer to question #2 is: **as long as you defend correctly, declarer is *not* going to make 3NT.**

You have now answered both questions and defended well to defeat 3NT. However, declarer could have played better.

He should have won the opening heart lead with *dummy's* ♡K. He needed to *save* his ♡A entry to get back to his clubs after he unblocked diamonds. He didn't need to save the ♡K to get back to North's diamonds – North's club holding was always going to provide an entry to the ◇J. If South had played that way, even *you* could not have prevented him from making nine tricks.

Here is the entire deal:

Contract: 3NT
Lead: ♡Q

North
♠ Q 8 7
♡ K 5 3
◇ J 5 4 2
♣ Q J 10

West (You)
♠ A 3 2
♡ Q J 10 9
◇ 9 7 6
♣ A 4 3

East
♠ K 5 4
♡ 8 7 6 2
◇ 10 8 3
♣ 8 6 2

South
♠ J 10 9 6
♡ A 4
◇ A K Q
♣ K 9 7 5

Know When To Hold 'Em

When declarer attacks a suit, it is often correct to duck even if you have *two* stoppers.

North
♠ K 6 5
♡ 6 3
◇ 7 4 3
♣ K 10 9 8 5

Contract: 3NT
Lead: ♠J

West
♠ J 10 9 7 4
♡ 8 7 2
◇ Q 10 8
♣ 7 2

East
♠ 8
♡ Q J 10 9
◇ J 9 6 2
♣ A Q 4 3

South
♠ A Q 3 2
♡ A K 5 4
◇ A K 5
♣ J 6

South won the first trick with his ♠Q and led the ♣J. If East wins, declarer is in control. He can win the obvious heart return and lead his ♣6 to knock out East's ♣A. South now has three club tricks, and will emerge with an overtrick.

East must duck the ♣J, and win the second club. Declarer no longer has a club to lead, and dummy's clubs are dead. South will take only three spades, two hearts, two diamonds and one club – down one.

Chapter 12

Creating Trump Tricks

Do You Believe in Magic?

When you create a trump trick out of thin air, you are delivering an *uppercut*. It is a nice word, but don't spend time memorizing it. I can't speak for others, but I'm a lot more impressed by a player who can execute this play rather than one who can only identify it by name.

Here's an opportunity for *you* to play Houdini.

Contract: 4♡
Lead: ♠A

North
♠ 9 6 5
♡ K Q 6 4
◇ A K J 9 7
♣ 3

West (You)
♠ A K Q J 3
♡ 9 7 2
◇ Q 10
♣ J 10 4

West	*North*	*East*	*South*
—	—	Pass	1♣
1♠	2◇	Pass	2♡
Pass	4♡	All Pass	

On your spade lead, partner signals with the ♠8. You continue with the ♠K and partner completes his high-low with the ♠4. Knowing that South has a third spade, at trick three, it's clear to cash the ♠Q.

On this trick, your partner makes the discouraging discard of the ♣2. Before reading on, decide what you would lead at the fourth trick.

What do you know at this point? When your partner discarded the ♣2, he clearly denied having the ♣A. In addition to your side's not having a club trick, the combination of dummy's imposing diamonds and your ♢Q 10 doubleton make it very clear that the defense will never win a diamond trick.

Despite your modest heart holding, your only hope is to create a trump trick. You should lead a low spade to make it clear to partner that you want him to ruff.

Dummy discards a diamond and partner ruffs with the ♡10, which forces declarer to overruff with the ace. This leaves the following position in trumps:

	North	
	♡ K Q 6 4	
West (You)		*East*
♡ 9 7 2		♡ J
	South	
	♡ 8 5 3	

Although declarer did nothing wrong (except sit down to play against *you*), he had to go down one. You and partner collaborated very nicely to create a trump trick out of thin air.

Here is the entire deal:

Contract: 4♡
Lead: ♠A

North
♠ 9 6 5
♡ K Q 6 4
◇ A K J 9 7
♣ 3

West (You)
♠ A K Q J 3
♡ 9 7 2
◇ Q 10
♣ J 10 4

East
♠ 8 4
♡ J 10
◇ 6 5 4 3
♣ 9 7 6 5 2

South
♠ 10 7 2
♡ A 8 5 3
◇ 8 2
♣ A K Q 8

West	*North*	*East*	*South*
—	—	Pass	1♣
1♠	2◇	Pass	2♡
Pass	4♡	All Pass	

Dreaming of an Eight-Spot

As in all competitive endeavors, you must remember not to throw in the towel when the outlook appears to be hopeless. This strategy is easy to understand but not always easy to apply. With a little practice, forging ahead and making something out of nothing can become a vital part of your philosophy.

When declarer has no losers in the *side suits*, the defenders should try to create a trump trick.

Consider the following:

Contract: 4♠
Lead: ♡A

North
♠ J 10 9
♡ 7 6 4
♢ K Q
♣ A K Q J 6

West (You)
♠ Q 7
♡ A K Q J 8 3
♢ A J 10 2
♣ 9

West	*North*	*East*	*South*
—	—	—	3♠
4♡	4♠	All Pass	

You were not thrilled about bidding 4♡ by yourself, but what else could you do? However, North was always bidding 4♠ based on his strong hand and more-than-adequate spade support. You sensibly decided that you had done your all and passed 4♠. That makes it your lead.

With an easy heart lead, you put your club singleton on hold. On your ♡A opening lead, East follows with the ♡9 and South plays the ♡5. Once partner encourages hearts without any high cards in the suit, it's clear that he started with a singleton or doubleton, so you are sure that a second heart will cash.

In fact, if partner's ♡9 was a singleton, South must have started with three hearts, and you'll be able to win three heart tricks. As long as South is not void in diamonds, you have a sure set.

However, when you cash the ♡K at the second trick, East and South both follow – which accounts for the missing hearts. Oh well, you'll have to be content with two heart tricks.

At this point, you're not very hopeful. It's not clear where your four tricks might come from.

What is your best chance to defeat the 4♠ contract? Plan your defense before reading on.

Dummy's club holding looks formidable, so your first step should be to grab the ♢A. Everyone follows. Now what?

You have no hope of winning another trick in hearts, clubs, or diamonds, so you need to win a spade trick. You know that South has seven spades for his preempt and you see five additional spades between your hand and dummy's. Therefore, your partner is marked with exactly one spade. If he has the ace or king, South has no chance. But suppose East's spade is not an honor.

When we were beginners, we were all taught: when searching for a trump suit, "eight is enough." Some of us also remember the television program of that name. Nevertheless, on this hand, if East's singleton trump happens to be the eight, it must be enough – as long as you make sure that partner ruffs.

You desperately want East to ruff, so at trick 4, lead the ♡3 to make it easy for him to do the right thing. As you can see on the actual hand, East does have the ♠8. When he ruffs with that card, it forces South to overruff with the king, and your ♠Q 7 is then good for the setting trick.

Here is the entire deal:

Contract: 4♠
Lead: ♡A

North
♠ J 10 9
♡ 7 6 4
♢ K Q
♣ A K Q J 6

West (You)
♠ Q 7
♡ A K Q J 8 3
♢ A J 10 2
♣ 9

East
♠ 8
♡ 9 2
♢ 9 8 7 5 4 3
♣ 5 4 3 2

South
♠ A K 6 5 4 3 2
♡ 10 5
♢ 6
♣ 10 8 7

West	*North*	*East*	*South*
—	—	—	3♠
4♡	4♠	All Pass	

Although your partner won't always have the perfect cards, these hands do occur. You may not believe in magic, but you should believe in uppercuts.

The Waiting Game

When you have an opportunity to overruff with a sure trump trick — don't.

This guideline has *very* few exceptions.

On these diagrams, spades are trump and East leads.

	North	
	♠ 5 4	
	♡ 8 6	
West		*East*
♠ A 10 9		♠ 6 2
♡ —		♡ 10 9
◇ 7		
	South	
	♠ K Q J 8	
	♡ —	

East leads the ♡10. When South ruffs with the ♠J, West must NOT overruff – he should discard the ◇7. The trump suit will now look like this:

	North	
	♠ 5 4	
West		*East*
♠ A 10 9		♠ 6 2
	South	
	♠ K Q 8	

West is now assured of two trump tricks.

Chapter 13

Sometimes, Longer *Is* Better

Hustler's Delight

If winning is not important, then tell me –
why keep score?

Klingon crew member
from *Star Trek, Next Generation*

I'd like to show you the hand of a lifetime. Imagine that you're playing in a team game and with both sides vulnerable, you are dealt the following monster:

♠ A K Q ♡ A K Q J 10 9 ◇ — ♣ A K Q J

Wow! Not only must this be the best hand that you have ever held, but even if you play bridge for another 50 years, I'll bet that you will never have a better one. You choose to open 7♡, which must be laydown.

You are surprised and delighted when West doubles; how naïve of your LHO to believe that he will defeat you with his ◇A. In fact, it's even insulting. You lose no time in redoubling, wondering if anyone is capable of figuring out the score (using duplicate scoring, it turns out to be 2940).

As expected, your LHO leads the ◇A. Dummy apologizes for his worthless hand, but you assure him that you have everything under control.

You ruff the opening lead, and begin drawing trumps. Your hearts are so awesome that even a 5-2 split will cause you no harm.

However, when you cash the ♡A, East shows out! And, when you try to take some of your winners in clubs and spades, West ruffs every single one of them!

Believe it or not, all you can take is six trump tricks! Every time West ruffs one of your black-suit winners, he plays another diamond, forcing you to trump. Having lost control of the hand, you are down seven, an impossible-to-imagine score of -4000.

Actually, with repeated diamond leads, your side cannot make any game contract. Unbelievable!

This infamous deal is obviously rigged. South is the pigeon to be plucked, preferably in a high-stakes rubber bridge game. In bridge circles, this is known as the Mississippi Heart Hand, because it was widely used by 19th century whist-playing card-sharps on Mississippi River steamboats.

In fact, legend has it that Charles M. Schwab lost at least $10,000 when he was the unlucky recipient of the too-good-to-be-true South hand.

Rigged or not, this deal does illustrate three important bridge concepts:

1. Points, schmoints!
2. The benefits of forcing declarer to trump.
3. Sometimes, length is more important than strength. After observing the fate of West's seven low hearts versus South's six high ones, case closed.

Contract: 7♡ Rdbl
Lead: ♢A

North
♠ 10 5 4 3 2
♡ —
♢ 5 4 3 2
♣ 5 4 3 2

West
♠ —
♡ 8 7 6 5 4 3 2
♢ A K Q J 10 9
♣ —

East
♠ J 9 8 7 6
♡ —
♢ 8 7 6
♣ 10 9 8 7 6

South (You)
♠ A K Q
♡ A K Q J 10 9
♢ —
♣ A K Q J

West	*North*	*East*	*South*
—	—	—	7♡
Dbl	Pass	Pass	Rdbl
All Pass			

Force Declarer to Trump – Absolutely!

The opponents bid to a contract of 4♠. You lead the ◇A, partner encourages with the 10 as declarer drops the jack. Here is the layout of the diamonds in view:

	North	
	◇ 7 5 4 3	
You		*Partner*
◇ A K 8 2		◇ 10
	South	
	◇ J	

You are delighted to continue with the king, but declarer trumps with the ♠2. Which of the following best expresses your feelings?

1. You wish you had shifted to another suit.
2. You are angry with partner for encouraging diamonds without a singleton or doubleton.
3. You regret allowing declarer to win a trick with his deuce of trumps. You'd take it back if you could.
4. You are pleased to have shortened declarer's trumps.

Too many players respond with a combination of the first three answers. Why is that? They channel their hopes and energy into winning the next trick. If they are not able to win that trick, they have failed. In their minds, that's all that counts.

You should not allow yourself to think this way. Defensive play must be considered from a long-range perspective. Declarer's losers won't magically disappear. On many hands, a patient attitude is the best approach.

As for how you *should* feel when declarer ruffs your lead without you setting up any of dummy's cards, here is a fundamental principle of good defense: **The defenders should usually be eager to shorten declarer's trumps.**

Assuming that declarer probably has the trump length for his side, it is important to understand that most (if not all) of his trumps will always be good tricks. Declarer is usually not happy when forced to part with one of his precious trumps. Take a look at this healthy trump suit:

North
♠ 7 5 4

South
♠ K Q J 10 2

Declarer is always going to win four spade tricks while losing one. However, if South can be forced to ruff twice, he'll be reduced to only three trumps. If a defender started with four trumps, *his* last card will become a winner.

The defenders should continue to shorten declarer's trumps in the hope that he will eventually lose control of the hand. This defensive strategy is referred to as *the forcing game.* It is especially applicable when one defender holds four trumps or has reason to believe that his partner might.

On the other hand, declarer is normally delighted to ruff in the *short* hand. The tricks dummy can win by ruffing represent bonus trump tricks. Declarer must be careful to keep enough trumps in his hand to retain control. On most deals, this is critical. The reality is, **declarer is usually not eager to ruff in the hand with trump length**. It should come as no surprise that declarer's objectives are the opposite of those of the defenders'.

As for the actual deal, take a look at the next page.

Without the diamond continuation at trick two, South would not have a problem. He'd draw trumps and lose one diamond, one heart, and one spade trick.

Once West forced declarer to trump, South could not handle the 4-1 trump split. He led the ♠K, which also won. Declarer continued with the ♠Q, and East ducked again. Regardless of how South played, he was finished. Every time East gained the lead, he pumped declarer with diamonds, and East's fourth trump was destined to take the setting trick.

Here is the entire deal:

	North	
Contract: 4♠	♠ 7 5 4	
Lead: ♢A	♡ A K 5	
	♢ 7 5 4 3	
	♣ 10 9 6	
West		*East*
♠ 9		♠ A 8 6 3
♡ J 10 3		♡ Q 9 8 7
♢ A K 8 2		♢ Q 10 9 6
♣ 8 7 5 4 2		♣ 3
	South	
	♠ K Q J 10 2	
	♡ 6 4 2	
	♢ J	
	♣ A K Q J	

West	*North*	*East*	*South*
Pass	Pass	Pass	1♠
Pass	2♠	Pass	4♠
All Pass			

The Forcing Game – look for it wherever bridge is played. I am confident you will enjoy your role. Meanwhile, the unfortunate declarer will be reduced to playing the lead in *The Crying Game*.

Support for Everyone

Here's another opportunity to make the most of your trump length.

North
♠ 9
♡ 4
♢ 9 8 4 3 2
♣ 9 8 7 5 4 2

Contract: 4♠
Lead: ♡K

East (You)
♠ A K 8 2
♡ A 8 7 6 3
♢ J 5
♣ J 6

West	*North*	*East*	*South*
2♡	Pass	4♡	4♠
All Pass			

Quite an interesting auction. Not only do you have 5-card support for partner's major, but you also have an awfully good holding in South's major suit.

When dummy hits, you are delighted to see North's minor-suit yarborough with singletons in each major. It's nice to know that your side will win a heart trick.

Question 1: What card do you play at trick 1?

Question 2: If you win the ♡A, what do you lead at trick 2?

Question 1: What card do you play at trick 1?

Answer: You should overtake partner's ♡K with your ace. You have a good plan, so you should take control. **Marty Sez**: He who knows, goes.

What is that good plan? Stay tuned. I will explain at length when answering question 2.

Question 2: If you win the ♡A, what do you lead at trick 2?

Answer: You should lead another heart to force N-S to use up one of their trumps. The fact that you are deliberately giving declarer a ruff-sluff is not a problem. If declarer sluffs a loser and ruffs on the board, it is still impossible for him to make the hand. Here is declarer's actual hand:

♠Q J 10 7 6 5 ♡2 ◇A K Q ♣A K Q

Even if declarer could see your cards, he can't make the hand! If he ruffs the heart with dummy's ♠9, he will lose a battle of *strength.* His trumps will be headed by the ♠Q J 10 7, and when he leads trumps, he can't prevent your ♠8 from taking the setting trick.

If instead, he ruffs in his hand, he will lose a battle of *length*. He'll then have five trumps against your four. Each time you get in with a trump honor, you'll lead hearts. Eventually, you'll have more trumps than he does, and down he'll go.

As you can see, even without any minor-suit losers, declarer is helpless.

New Question: Did your intelligent defense guarantee the defeat of the contract?

Answer: Not quite. If declarer had a seventh spade instead of one of his minor-suit queens, he could trump the heart in his hand and have just enough trumps to limit you to two trump tricks.

Here is the entire deal:

North
♠ 9
♡ 4
♢ 9 8 4 3 2
♣ 9 8 7 5 4 2

Contract: 4♠
Lead: ♡K

West
♠ 4 3
♡ K Q J 10 9 5
♢ 10 7 6
♣ 10 3

East (You)
♠ A K 8 2
♡ A 8 7 6 3
♢ J 5
♣ J 6

South
♠ Q J 10 7 6 5
♡ 2
♢ A K Q
♣ A K Q

West	*North*	*East*	*South*
2♡	Pass	4♡	4♠
All Pass			

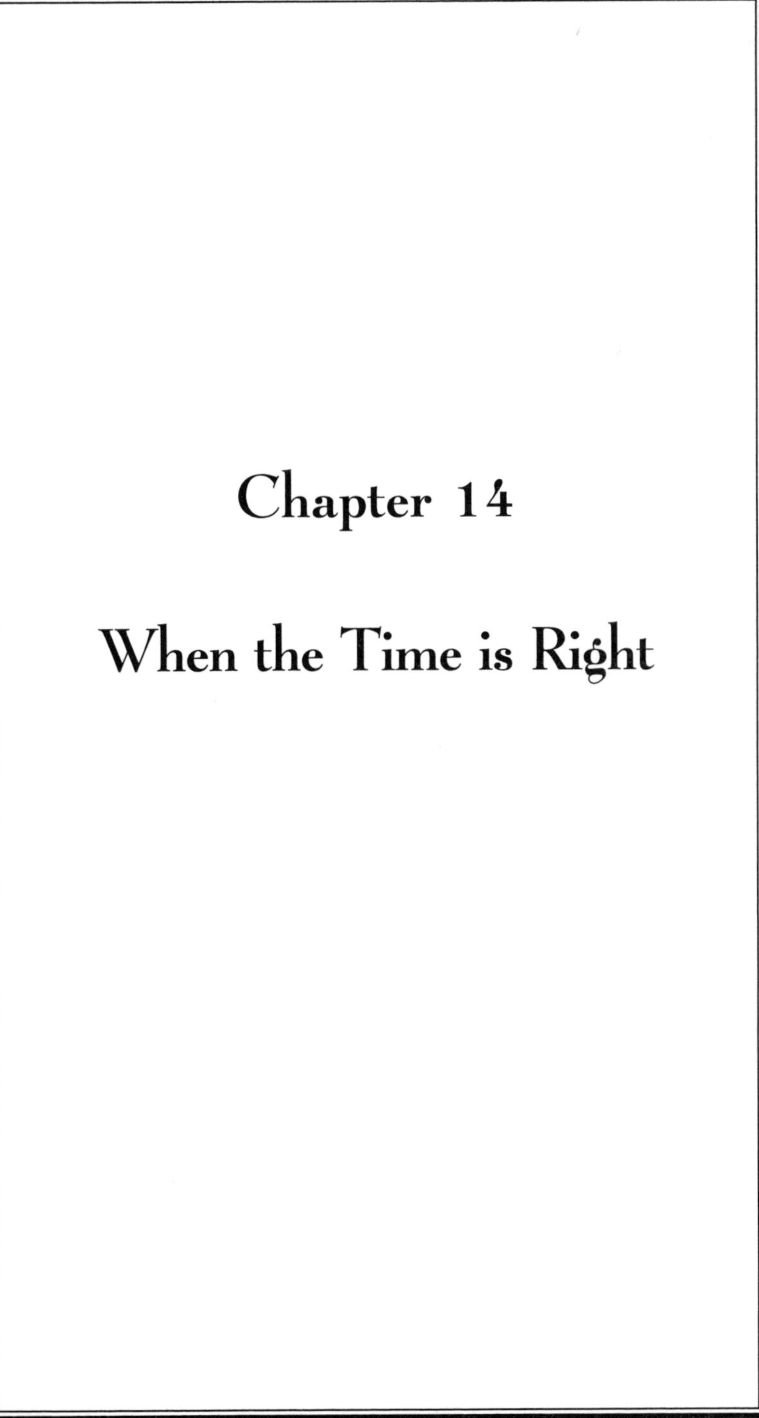

Chapter 14

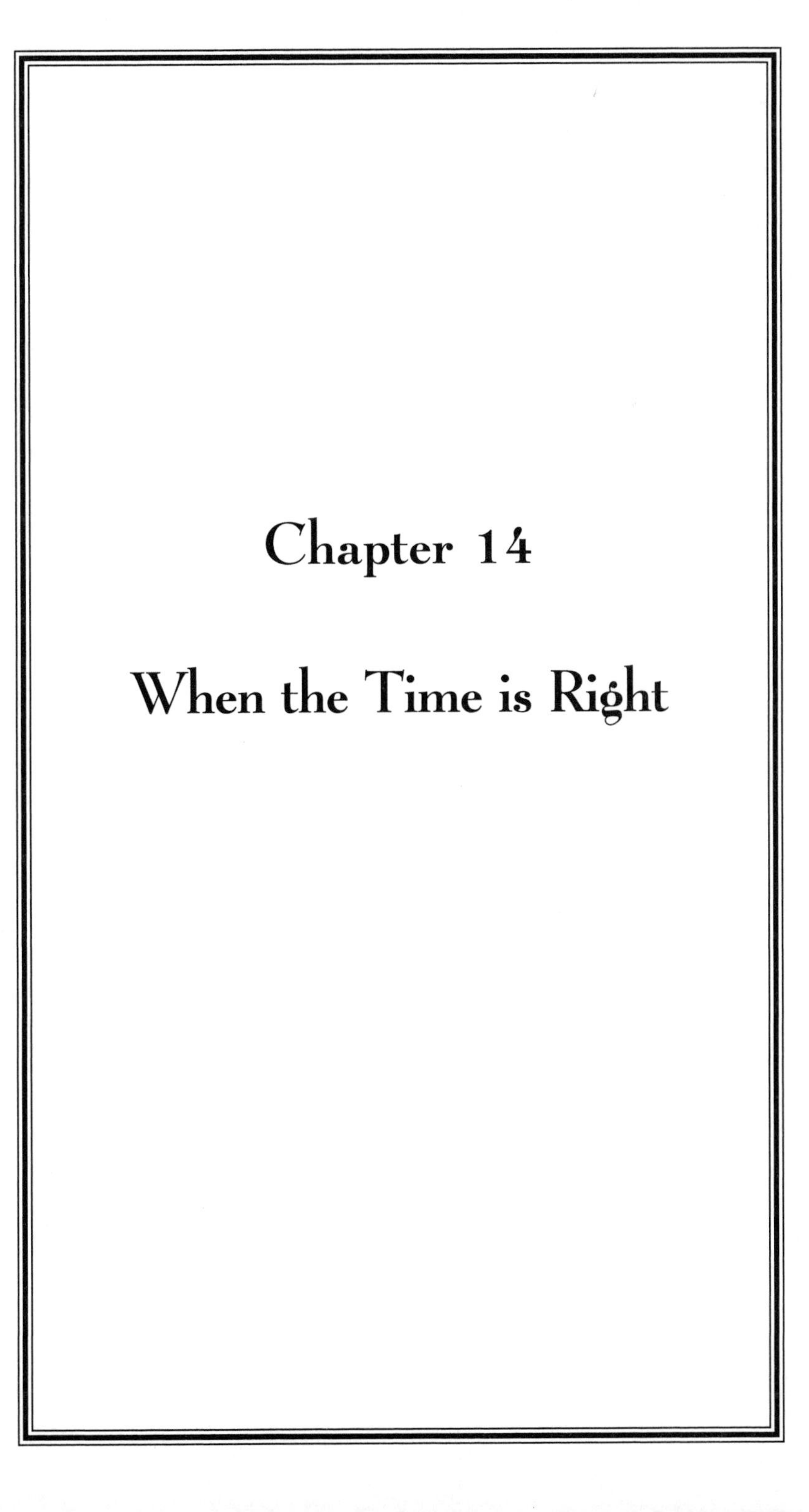

When the Time is Right

An Artist with a Small Canvas

"The ultimate in bridge is learning to play with poor hands."

Chip Martel, many-time World Champion

A bridge hand containing no card higher than a 9 is referred to as a yarborough, named after an English lord who would wager 1,000 pounds to one against the chance of being dealt such a hand.

Lord Yarborough certainly knew what he was doing. The actual odds of such a hand are 1827 to 1.

Nowadays, *yarborough* is used to describe a very bad hand, not necessarily adhering to the original requirements. Modern players would refer to the following hand as a yarborough:

♠ 8 6 5 ♡ 6 4 3 ◇ 9 7 2 ♣ 10 8 7 3

As I watched one of my best students pick up a really terrible hand, I could almost hear her thoughts.

"What a lousy hand," thought Jane as she gazed at:

♠ 8 6 5 4 3 ♡ 7 6 ◇ 2 ♣ 9 7 6 4 2

"I hope that partner opens 1♠; I'd love to jump to 4♠ and apply The Law of Total Tricks. Too bad, partner opened 1◇. So much for that. Sounds like a good time for a little snooze."

"Oh, the bidding is over already. Is it my lead? I'd love to lead my singleton. Nope, partner is on lead against 4♡. Oh well, back to sleep."

West leads the ♢A and dummy proudly tables:

♠A K Q J 9 ♡A K Q J ♢Q 5 ♣J 10

"Wow, quite a hand – 23 HCP! I'll bet declarer doesn't have much more than I do. Now partner is playing the ♢K; time for a discard. I should give her some information. I don't need to tell her that my spades are lousy, she can figure that out for herself."

"I guess I should tell her that I don't like clubs. I'll discard the two..."

"No, wait a minute! Wake up, Janie! It can't be right to leave partner on lead, what good would that do? Is there any hope? Maybe partner has the ♣A Q. In that case, I've gotta get in and lead a club. Guess it's now or never. Okay, ♡6, do your stuff."

There were surprised looks all around when Jane trumped her partner's ♢K. However, when she returned the ♣4, South looked *very* unhappy. Down one. With any other defense, declarer would have drawn trumps and discarded her clubs on dummy's spades.

"You trumped my trick, partner," said West. "Thank you!"

Here is the entire deal:

North
♠ A K Q J 9
♡ A K Q J
◇ Q 5
♣ J 10

Contract: 4♡
Lead: ◇A

West
♠ 7 2
♡ 5 2
◇ A K J 10 8 3
♣ A Q 8

East (Jane)
♠ 8 6 5 4 3
♡ 7 6
◇ 2
♣ 9 7 6 4 2

South
♠ 10
♡ 10 9 8 4 3
◇ 9 7 6 4
♣ K 5 3

West	*North*	*East*	*South*
1◇	Dbl	Pass	1♡
2◇	4♡	All Pass	

The Right Time to Cover

Cover an honor with an honor when:
you have a realistic chance to set up a trick for yourself or your partner.

This is definitely a lot to remember and understand. It's no wonder that most players are content to walk around chanting: "Cover an honor with an honor."

While the last statement is very easy to remember, on many hands it is totally absurd. For example:

You are East, defending a 4♠ contract after South opened 2♠ and North raised to game. Here are the trumps for you and dummy. (If you're curious about the other suits, don't worry, they are not relevant.)

North
♠Q 5 4 3

East (You)
♠K 2

Declarer wins partner's opening heart lead on the board and leads the ♠Q. To cover, or not to cover, that is the question.

With the bidding in mind, and the two hands in view, covering dummy's ♠Q with your ♠K can *never* gain. It would be an example of your being eager to play "Heads, I lose – tails I tie." How can you know this?

As usual, the answer is based on counting. South is known to have started with six spades. Dummy has four, and you have two.

Once you subtract from 13, you know that partner started with only one spade. Regardless of what his singleton is, there is obviously no way to promote anything for him. Meanwhile, covering with your king is certainly not going to promote your ♠2. Therefore, on this hand, you definitely should not "cover an honor with an honor."

In addition, when the ♠Q is led, you need to duck smoothly. If you stop to think it over, declarer will know that you have the king. However, if you can play low without hesitating, South will not know who has the king. This could pay huge dividends; after all, declarer might decide to go up with his ace. Many players mistakenly believe that, with ten cards missing the king, they should play for the drop.

By the way: Just in case a frisky opponent chose to open 2♠ with ♠ J 10 9 8 7 6, playing low avoids everyone's worst bridge nightmare – playing your trump king on the same trick as your partner's ace.

You Be The Judge – Act 2

Contract: 3NT
Lead: ♣4

North
♠ K J 10
♡ Q 10 9 8
◊ K J 6 4
♣ Q J

West
♠ 9 5 4
♡ 6 5 4 2
◊ 8
♣ A 7 6 4 3

East
♠ 8 7 3 2
♡ A K J
◊ 7 3 2
♣ K 9 8

South
♠ A Q 6
♡ 7 3
◊ A Q 10 9 5
♣ 10 5 2

West	*North*	*East*	*South*
—	—	—	1◊
Pass	1♡	Pass	1NT
Pass	3NT	All Pass	

Trick 1: ♣4 is won by East's king.

Trick 2: East returned the ♣9, and West played low.

After winning dummy's ♣Q, declarer claimed nine tricks. Obviously, the defense could have taken two clubs and three heart tricks.

When the smoke cleared, East blamed West, and West blamed East. I have some *very* strong opinions here (what else is new?), but first I'll give you a chance to play judge and jury. What do you think went wrong?

Most players blame West. I believe that very few players would duck their ♣A at trick two. Of course, even if West had won the ♣A, I can't imagine any logic that would dictate a heart shift.

Personally, I have nothing but praise for West's defense. From his point of view, clubs offered the only chance to beat the hand. When East returned the ♣9, West knew that South still had the ♣10, and was entitled to one club trick. West could have won the ♣A and knocked out declarer's ♣10, but that would have been an exercise in futility. West didn't have any chance of getting in again, so setting up two club winners for *himself* could not accomplish anything.

West hoped that East had started with three clubs. By giving declarer his inevitable club trick, West planned to run clubs as soon as East gained the lead. East was marked with points – it was just unlucky that declarer had nine fast tricks.

Go back to trick one. Once he won the ♣K, East was well-placed to defeat 3NT. All he needed was for West to lead a heart when he got in with the ♣A. The writing was on the wall; but East couldn't read it.

After winning the ♣K, East should have first led the ♡K (remember, only lead the ace from ace-king on opening lead). Then, and only then, should he return partner's club lead. After that start, I'm confident that West would have been delighted to grab his ♣A and return East's heart lead.

Moral of the story? When you know what is best, make sure that you let your partner in on the secret. After all, what fun is it to know a secret if nobody else knows you know it?

{deal repeated for convenience}

Contract: 3NT
Lead: ♣4

North
♠ K J 10
♡ Q 10 9 8
◇ K J 6 4
♣ Q J

West
♠ 9 5 4
♡ 6 5 4 2
◇ 8
♣ A 7 6 4 3

East
♠ 8 7 3 2
♡ A K J
◇ 7 3 2
♣ K 9 8

South
♠ A Q 6
♡ 7 3
◇ A Q 10 9 5
♣ 10 5 2

Chapter 15

Defeating Slams

The Killing Defense

Contract: 6♡
Lead: ♢Q

North
♠ A Q 10 6 5
♡ Q J 10
♢ 4 2
♣ J 6 4

East (You)
♠ K J 7 4
♡ 6 4 2
♢ A 8 7 6 5
♣ 10

West	*North*	*East*	*South*
—	—	—	1♡
Pass	1♠	Pass	3♣
Pass	4♡	Pass	4NT
Pass	5♢	Dbl	6♡
All Pass			

You win the opening lead of the ♢Q with your ace, as South drops the nine.

Question 1: What is your analysis?

Question 2: What would you lead at trick 2?

P.S. Don't be nervous. Only a slam is at stake.

Question 1: What is your analysis?

Answer: If South began with two spades, sooner or later he'll take the spade finesse and go down. Therefore, assume he has only one.

Don't bother dreaming of a club ruff. For his jump to 6♡, declarer must have the ♣A along with the ♡AK.

If declarer wants to ruff a diamond in dummy, you can't stop him. What *can* you stop him from doing? **If he needs to set up dummy's fifth spade by using dummy's three trump entries, you can stop *that*!**

Question 2: What would you lead at trick 2?

Answer: The correct lead is a trump, which removes one of dummy's entries. After your trump shift, South can't set up dummy's fifth spade and can't make 6♡.

On the other hand, if you lead a minor suit at trick 2, declarer will win the trick and continue as follows:

Trick 3: Lead the ♠8 to dummy's ace.

Trick 4: Ruff a spade with the ♡8.

Trick 5: Lead the ♡3 to dummy's ♡10.

Trick 6: Ruff another spade with the ♡9.

Trick 7: Lead the ♡5 to dummy's ♡J.

Trick 8: Ruff a spade, which removes East's ♠K.

Trick 9: Lead ♡7 to ♡Q, which also draws trumps.

Trick 10: Discard the ♣9 on dummy's last spade.

Here is the entire deal:

	North	
Contract: 6♡	♠ A Q 10 6 5	
Lead: ◊Q	♡ Q J 10	
	◊ 4 2	
	♣ J 6 4	
West		*East* (You)
♠ 9 3 2		♠ K J 7 4
♡ —		♡ 6 4 2
◊ Q J 10 3		◊ A 8 7 6 5
♣ Q 8 7 5 3 2		♣ 10
	South	
	♠ 8	
	♡ A K 9 8 7 5 3	
	◊ K 9	
	♣ A K 9	

West	*North*	*East*	*South*
—	—	—	1♡
Pass	1♠	Pass	3♣
Pass	4♡	Pass	4NT
Pass	5◊	Dbl	6♡
All Pass			

Are You Endplayed?

	North
Contract: 6♠	♠ Q 10 9 4 3
Lead: ♡10	♡ K J
	◊ K 4
	♣ K 7 4 3

West (You)
♠ K 2
♡ 10 9 8 2
◊ Q 8 7 6 3
♣ J 6

West	*North*	*East*	*South*
—	—	—	1♠
Pass	2NT*	3♡	4♡
Pass	4♠	Pass	6♠
All Pass			

2NT* = Jacoby 2NT, promising an opening bid (or better) with at least 4-card support for spades.

Declarer covers your ♡10 lead with dummy's jack and East plays the ♡Q. You are disappointed but not surprised when South ruffs. On this auction, cue-bidding the enemy suit *should* promise a void.

At trick two, South cashes the ♠A, and your partner discards a heart. Two voids on one deal; that doesn't happen every day.

Declarer leads the ♢9 to dummy's king, and East follows with the two. South then leads the ♡K from the board. East covers with the ace and declarer ruffs.

South cashes the ♢A as everyone follows with small cards. When South leads the ♢10, you play low. Declarer ruffs it in dummy, and partner plays the ♢J.

At trick 7, declarer leads a trump from the board. Your partner discards another heart, and you win the ♠K. It is now your lead. Here is the position:

West (You)
♠ —
♡ 9 8
♢ Q 8
♣ J 6

Please select your lead before reading on.

Marty Sez hint: A defender who counts has a much better chance of doing the right thing than one who does not.

If you led a club, I have good news and bad news. The good news is that you will be receiving two nice gifts at holiday time. The bad news is that:

1. the gifts will be courtesy of your opponents;
2. you will definitely not be receiving any gifts from your partner;
3. as I'm sure you have figured out by the above, you just handed declarer his slam.

On the other hand, if you gave declarer a ruff-sluff by leading a red card (any one will do) – congratulations, you have just defeated the contract.

Why is that? What did you learn about South's shape when you counted his hand? At the first trick, you knew that declarer was void in hearts. When partner didn't follow to the first round of trumps, that meant that declarer started with six spades. Because declarer was dealt six cards in the majors, he must have begun the hand with seven cards in the minors.

When South and East followed to three rounds of diamonds, all 13 cards of that suit were accounted for. Therefore, you're sure that declarer has four clubs, and that should be all the information you need. At this point, you don't have to figure out who has the missing honors. **As long as both declarer and dummy have four clubs, a ruff-sluff can't possibly help declarer.**

As you can see, if you lead a red card, declarer will still have to lose a club. However, if you lead a club, you will destroy partner's club holding and the slam will come home. No, you were not endplayed.

Here is the entire deal:

North
♠ Q 10 9 4 3
♡ K J
◇ K 4
♣ K 7 4 3

Contract: 6♠
Lead: ♡10

West (You)
♠ K 2
♡ 10 9 8 2
◇ Q 8 7 6 3
♣ J 6

East
♠ —
♡ A Q 7 6 5 4 3
◇ J 5 2
♣ Q 9 2

South
♠ A J 8 7 6 5
♡ —
◇ A 10 9
♣ A 10 8 5

West	*North*	*East*	*South*
—	—	—	1♠
Pass	2NT*	3♡	4♡
Pass	4♠	Pass	6♠
All Pass			

2NT* = Jacoby 2NT

The Leading Question

Lead passively against a grand slam or 6NT.
Lead aggressively against all other slam contracts.

Your goal against grand slams:

Make the safest lead possible, which is often a trump. Obvious logical exception: if you think that the opponents might be missing an ace, or that partner might have a void, you should try to "find" him.

Your goal against 6NT:

In general, prefer to make a passive lead to avoid giving anything away. Obviously, leading the top of a 3-card sequence is your first choice.

If both opponents have shown balanced hands, a top of nothing lead is just fine. However, if either opponent has promised a long suit, you should prefer to make an aggressive lead.

Your goal against a small slam in a suit:

Set up trick(s) for your side before declarer can discard his losers. Lead very aggressively. This is often the right time to lay down an ace or lead away from a king or queen. You should usually avoid making a passive trump lead.

Bergenisms

Chapter 1 - Getting Off on the Right Foot

Page #

15. The purpose of cheapest of equals is to give information to your partner about your holding in a particular suit.

15. In a cheapest of equals situation, the play of any card denies possession of the adjacent lower card.

16. Cheapest of equals only applies when a defender plays third or fourth to the trick.

18. The only time you can give a signal is when you're free to do so because you are not involved in competing for the trick.

19. The easiest signal to give is count.

19. When declarer leads a suit, a defender should give count to let his partner know whether he has an odd or even number of cards in that suit.

20. Suit-preference signals are given when you want partner to lead a specific suit.

Chapter 2 - Attitude Problems

Page #

23. When making a discard, letting partner know which suit you don't like is often a better approach than signaling which suit you do like. This allows you to hold on to your good cards.

23. When defending a notrump contract, it is especially important to hold on to the suit you are trying to establish.

25. Never signal with a card that might take a trick if you hold on to it.

27. Even if partner's lead promises the AK, don't always high-low with a doubleton. Encourage *only* if you *want* him to continue the suit.

27. When you have a sure trump trick, don't look to use it for ruffs.

28. Respect partner's signals. He knows more about his hand than you do.

29. No matter how good you think your instincts are, bridge is a *partnership game.* Trusting partner's bids and signals should always take priority.

Chapter 3 - Count Signals

Page #

33. I recommend helping partner by almost always giving count.

34. When giving count, with an even number of cards (usually 2 or 4), start with the *highest* card you are sure you can afford. With an odd number (usually 3 or 5 cards), begin with your *lowest* one.

34. When partner gives count, you must:
    - notice and remember it;
    - decide if his card is high or low;
    - analyze how many cards partner has;
    - subtract to know how many declarer has;
    - then take the appropriate action.

36. When declarer tries to set up dummy's suit, wait until declarer is playing his last card in the suit before you take your winner.

36. When trying to figure out the distribution of the concealed hands, look for clues from the bidding as well as the first few tricks.

38. Although giving count can help in many situations, the most important ones are those where the defenders have to decide when to release their stopper.

Chapter 4 - Suit Preference Signals

Page #

43. When you are giving partner a ruff, or attempting to do so, a suit-preference signal is given with the card you lead for him to ruff.

46. Leading a singleton is especially attractive when you have trump control.

46. With a choice between leading a singleton or an AK combination, leading the ace is more flexible. You get to see dummy as well as partner's signal. *You* then have the ability to lead whatever seems best.

47. In a suit contract, when dummy has a singleton in the suit you led, if your partner is free to signal, it is not an attitude signal, it is suit-preference.

50. Suit-preference signals can also be used when you are knocking out declarer's last stopper to set up your suit in notrump, and you want to let partner know where your entry is.

Chapter 5 - Applying the Rule of 11

Page #

55. Any time you think that your partner has made a 4th-best lead, you should apply the Rule of 11.

55. The Rule of 11 *does* apply in both notrump and suit contracts - as long as the lead is 4th-best.

55. The Rule of 11 applies on any 4th-best lead, not just on opening lead.

56. The lead of a high spot card usually reveals more about declarer's cards than the lead of a low card.

56. The Rule of 11 doesn't help the opening leader, but is invaluable for his partner.

56. If the Rule of 11 contradicts the cards in view, you can be sure that partner led top of nothing, rather than 4th-best.

56. Don't lead 4th-best if you can lead the top of a sequence.

58. If you get a chance to clarify matters for partner, make things crystal clear.

Chapter 6 -Notrump Opening Leads

Page #

68. When you're on lead against notrump, a suit such as Q J 9 x *is* considered a sequence, even though it is headed by only two consecutive cards. The key is that there is a gap of just 1 card before the next card.

69. The following are also considered to be $2\frac{1}{2}$ card sequences, so lead 10 from 10 9 7 x, jack from J 10 8 x, and king from K Q 10 x.

69. A sequence must contain at least one honor, and the 10 is the lowest honor card. So, 10 9 8 is a sequence, but 9 8 7 is not.

73. If partner has a chance to make a lead-directing double of an artificial bid, but doesn't, his pass denies length and strength in that suit. So, if you need to "find" him, look elsewhere.

74. Even in notrump, avoid an opening lead from a 4-card suit headed by the ace (without the king). Of course, if partner promised length in the suit, you'll be happy, as always, to lead partner's suit.

Chapter 7 - Leading Trumps

Page #

77. When you have unattractive holdings in all 3 side suits, you should usually lead a trump.

78. Also lead trump when dummy is known to be short in a side suit. One example of a known short suit is an auction where the dummy denied support for his partner's major-suit opening bid.

79. Analyzing the opponent's auction is essential when considering your opening lead.

80. In general, don't lead a singleton trump.

80. When the opponents sacrifice, almost always lead trump - even with a singleton.

82. When the opponents have limited strength, their only hope for tricks is distribution, so lead trumps early and often.

84. These auctions also call for trump leads:

    - when your side opens 1NT, and you are on lead against a 2-suited auction;
    - when partner passes your takeout double of an opening bid of 1♣ or 1♢.

Chapter 8 - More Opening Leads

Page #

88. When declarer promised a very long trump suit, an attacking lead is the way to go.

88. When an aggressive lead is called for, leading from a king is better than leading from a queen, and both are better than leading from a jack.

90. When you are leading from xxx or xxxx in a notrump contract, if partner never showed the suit, lead high - top of nothing.

91. When leading partner's suit in notrump *after* you showed support, but have only small cards, lead high.

91. When leading partner's suit in notrump from a holding of xxx or xxxx, but you *never* showed support:

    - if partner promised 5+ cards, lead low;
    - if partner might have 4 cards, lead high.

91. After seeing dummy, you might not lead the same card you would choose on opening lead. New situations often require new strategy.

92. In a suit contract, every pair must agree on which card to lead from a worthless suit. Choices are: low, MUD, or top of nothing.

Chapter 9 - Counting

Page #

99. Counting distribution is one of the abilities that distinguishes bridge players from BRIDGE PLAYERS.

99. When counting declarer's distribution: if he opens a minor, the only way he can have a 5-card major is if he later bids *and rebids* that suit.

101. As soon as dummy is tabled, each defender should add dummy's HCP to his own. By keeping the auction in mind, you may be able to zero in on the remaining HCP. This is easiest to apply when the auction pinpoints declarer's HCP, such as when he opens 1NT.

102. Use up the honor from the short side first (to unblock) is just as important for the defenders as it is for declarer.

103. The fact than an opponent bids a suit does not mean that the defense should *never* lead it.

104. When a player bids three suits, there is a good chance that he has a singleton in the fourth suit.

Chapter 10 - Partnership Defense

Page #

112. Never underlead an ace at trick one against a suit contract.

113. Concentrate all your energy on the hand - not on rationalizing in the post-mortem.

113. At trick 1 in a suit contract, if dummy does not have the ace, third-hand's play of the jack from a suit that includes the KJ has a lot of merit. This discovery play will allow you to immediately know who has the queen.

114-116. If you'd like to be a desirable partner:

- do not give lessons.
- don't say anything to your partner unless you'd want him to say the same to you.
- never criticize partner for a normal action just because it didn't work out.
- don't discuss the hand just played *now*.
- always remember that you and partner are on the same side.
- never embarrass your partner in front of others.
- always trust your partner.
- remember, bridge is just a card game.
- last but not least, have a good time.

Chapter 11 - Entry Killing

Page #

120. At the first trick, third-hand should always try to figure out what his partner and declarer are likely to have in the suit that was just led.

120. When dummy has a long suit but only one outside entry, the defenders want to go to great lengths to knock out that entry *before* declarer can set up the long suit.

122. After leading the top card in a sequence, it is normal to continue by playing the bottom card.

124. As the hand evolves, the defenders should try to keep track of declarer's high cards. By zeroing in on declarer's HCP, each defender may be able to figure out who has the missing honors.

126. When declarer attacks a suit, it is often correct to duck even if you have *two* stoppers in that suit.

Chapter 12 - Creating Trump Tricks

Page #

132. Even if your situation appears to be hopeless, never throw in the towel. Because this game is so difficult, miracles (and accidents) do occur.

132. When declarer has no losers remaining in the side suits, the defenders should try to create a trump trick.

134. Anyone can win tricks with aces and kings. However, one of the most important qualities that separates the best players from the masses is the ability to get the most out of lesser cards. Cards such as eights, nines and tens are often relevant.

134. When leading a suit where partner is void, make your intentions totally clear to him. If you want him to ruff, lead a low card. If you don't want him to ruff, lead high.

135. Although partner won't always have the perfect cards, you can create trump tricks for your side. You may not believe in magic, but you should believe in uppercuts.

136. When you have a chance to *overruff* with a sure trump trick - don't.

Chapter 13 - Sometimes, Longer is Better

Page #

141. A defender who has *length* in trumps can create a lot of headaches for declarer, even if those trumps lack *strength.*

142. Too many players channel their hopes and energy into winning the next trick. If they are not able to win that trick, they believe they have failed. Don't allow yourself to think this way.

143. Good defense must be considered from a long-range perspective. Declarer's losers won't magically disappear. On many hands, a patient approach is the best policy.

143. The defenders should usually be eager to shorten declarer's trumps. That will make it more difficult for declarer to draw trumps and maintain control.

147. When you have a good plan, you should take control. He who knows, goes.

Chapter 14 - When the Time is Right

Page #

151. *"The ultimate in bridge is learning to play with poor hands."*

152. Obviously, on most hands, you should not trump your partner's winning trick. On the other hand, when it is crucial for you to get the lead, you gotta do what you gotta do.

154. "Cover an honor with an honor only when you have a realistic chance to promote something for yourself or your partner." That is accurate. The simpler statement, "Cover an honor with an honor," is not.

155. If you decide not to cover when an honor is led through you, it is best if you can duck smoothly. If you stop to think it over, declarer will know you have the honor. If possible, make your decision in advance.

157. When a defender wants to set up his long suit in notrump, but has limited entries, a duck may be the perfect answer.

158. After trick one, the normal lead from a suit that includes the king and ace is the *king.*

Chapter 15 - Defeating Slams

Page #

162. If a defender has the opportunity to use up dummy's entries early in the hand, that is often the best defense.

166. Once you have counted three suits, figuring out the fourth suit should be easy.

166. Almost always, the last thing a defender wants to do is give declarer a ruff-sluff. On the other hand, if declarer *definitely* has no loser to discard, giving him a ruff-sluff may very well represent a defender's best option.

168. General guidelines for leading aqainst slams:

    - vs. a grand slam – your goal is to make the safest lead possible, which is often a trump.

    - vs. 6NT – make a passive lead to avoid giving anything away.

    - vs. a small slam in a suit – set up trick(s) for your side before declarer has a chance to discard his losers.
      Lead very aggressively.

Bidding Highlights

Page #

38. With a balanced hand and the appropriate point count, you can't wait for stoppers in all suits to open 1NT or 2NT.

47. When partner makes a takeout double, all jumps below game are invitational, and show approximately 10 points, including distribution.

70. After opening the bidding in a minor suit, if opener jumps in the same minor at his second turn, he denies having four cards in either major.

73. If you have enough length and strength to make a lead-directing double of an artificial bid, be sure to double. If you fail to, your partner will shy away from leading that suit.

98. Once you have found a fit, the value of a void increases dramatically. You can often make a game or slam without a lot of HCP.

100. Responder needs six cards to rebid his suit, so even if he never does, a 5-3 fit is still possible. Therefore, if opener has 3-card support, sooner or later, he should show that support.

Bidding Highlights...continued

Page #

100. If you find a major-suit fit, do not look for a fit in another suit.

108. With a suitable hand, opener should be willing to immediately raise responder's major with only 3-card support.

109. An overcall in a 4-card suit should be based on at least three honors in that suit.

114. Learn your partner's style, even if you don't always agree with it.

116. Do not expect your partner to bid exactly as you would. When partner makes a bid, consider what *he'll* have, not what you would.

116. Don't throw tricky bids at partner. Seek the bid that will make his life easy.

122. If you're lucky enough to find yourself on lead against 3NT with Q J 10 9 x and two aces, don't forget to double.

129. Good hands bid naturally - longest suit first. Weak or mediocre hands must be practical, and bid the most important suit first.

Bidding Highlights...continued

Page #

129. Don't make a negative double if you have a bid available that will allow you to accurately describe your hand. Negative Doubles is a terrific convention, but if you don't need it - don't use it.

151. The Law of Total Tricks recommends competing to the level of your sides' total number of trumps, even with weak hands. Of course, in following The LAW, you must not lie to your partner about your strength.

160. One of the most important opportunities to make a lead-directing double is when your RHO is responding to Blackwood.

164. When responder wants to make a forcing raise in opener's major suit, Jacoby 2NT is an excellent convention to look for slam. The bid promises an opening bid (or better) with at least 4-card support.

164. Because a Jacoby 2NT auction is forcing to game, if an opponent interferes, a pass is forcing. Therefore, taking up bidding room by cue-bidding the opponent's suit is only justified when you have a void in that suit.

Declarer Highlights

Page #

39. If declarer has a solid suit that he never bid, he may be better off *not* cashing those tricks early in the play. This approach may succeed in lulling the defenders into a false sense of security.

60. Declarer should usually play the highest of equal cards when competing for tricks or capturing them. Because he has no interest in communicating with *his* partner during the play, it's not surprising that his optimum strategy is the opposite of what he would do as a defender.

119. When a defender's lead marks declarer with a specific card, he should play that card ASAP (unless, of course, it costs a trick). Holding on to a card you are known to have is the equvalent of allowing the defenders to look at your hand.

123. On most hands where declarer's key suit is blocked, he must unblock that suit ASAP.

125. When declarer has a choice of where to win a trick, the key is usually not where he needs to be now; it is where he will need to be later on.

Declarer Highlights...continued

Page #

144. Declarer is eager to ruff in the hand that has fewer trumps, but is usually not thrilled when he is forced to ruff in the hand with trump length.

155. Because many opponents will almost always "cover an honor with an honor," declarer can take advantage of the enemy by leading an honor through them as often as he can. Even if the opponent does not cover, declarer may be able to gain information by observing the body language.

155. Inducing your opponents to crash their honors is *very* satisfying.

163. Any time dummy has a five cards in a side suit, declarer should consider setting up the suit. Very often, the key factor is: how many entries dummy has in the other suits.

165. Whether or not you have a legitimate opportunity for an endplay, stripping the side suits before throwing in an opponent represents good technique.

Defender's Glossary Plus

2½ Card Sequence – A Bergenism which reminds players that the proper card to lead in notrump from a holding such as Q J 9 8 is the top card – in this case, the queen.

Attacking Lead – A risky lead from 1 or 2 honors in an aggressive attempt to win or establish tricks.

Attitude Signal – A way to tell partner if you like the suit he led. A high card encourages, while a low card discourages. Also used when you are void in the suit led, regardless of which side led the suit.

Blocked Suit – A suit in which it is impossible to immediately cash all the winning cards.
For example, AQ opposite Kxx.

Blocking a Suit – A play which results in a blocked suit. Blocking the opponents' suit is highly recommended; blocking your suit is not.

Board – Dummy's hand. *On the board* means that the previous trick was won by dummy's hand.

Break a Suit – Slang for leading a new suit after the first trick. Many players are too eager to break suits.

Capture – Playing a high card to take a trick away from an opponent.

Card Sense – Having a special aptitude for playing card games.

Cash – Leading a winning card to take the trick.

Cheapest of Equals – A technique used by a defender when he is competing for a trick. Play the lowest card that will either capture the trick or not allow declarer to win a trick with a small card.

Communication (Transportation) – The ability to win tricks in either defender's hand. If the partnership assets are not evenly divided, limited communication can result in entry problems.

Competing for the Trick – Trying to win the trick, as well as ensuring that declarer can't win it cheaply.

Counting – One of the abilities that separates BRIDGE PLAYERS from bridge players. Good defenders always count: distribution, HCP, tricks, etc.

Count Signal – A way to tell partner about your length in the suit led by declarer. Like all signals, it only applies if you are not involved in competing for the trick, With an even number of cards, signal with the highest card you can afford. When you have an odd number, begin with your lowest one.

"Cover an Honor with an Honor"– This slogan is very popular and easy to remember, but *very misleading.* Instead, you should cover only when you have a realistic chance to set up a trick for yourself or your partner.

Crashing Honors – Costing your side a trick by wasting two honors on the same trick. This is the defenders' worst nightmare.

Crossruff – A line of play in which ruffing tricks are made in both partner's hands on an alternating basis. The best defense against declarer's crossruff is to lead trumps early and often.

Develop - See *Set Up*.

Discard – Throwing off a card in any suit except trumps when you are void in the suit led.

Discovery Play – A play made to learn more about the opponent's hand.

Double Dummy Defense – A hand that was defended perfectly, as though the player was able to look at all four hands.

Drive Out – Forcing an opponent to take a trick with his winning card to set up tricks for your side.

Duck – Playing a small card to surrender a trick you could have won now, but would prefer to win later. A player *ducks* in order to save his entry to set up his own suit, but *holds up* to make it difficult for the opponents to set up their suit.

Entry – Any card that allows you to gain the lead in a particular hand.

Entry-Killing Play – A play made to deny declarer access to either his hand or the dummy.

Establish – See *Set Up.*

Exit – Making a safe lead that gives the lead back to declarer.

Falsecard – Playing a card with the express purpose of deceiving declarer.

Finesse – A maneuver to try to win a trick with a card that is not yet a winner. Being able to see one of the opponent's hands (the dummy) may enable a defender to finesse with confidence.

Forcing Game – A defensive strategy of intentionally leading declarer's short suit to force him to ruff and shorten his trumps. If the defense can force declarer often enough, he may lose control of the hand.

4th-Best Leads – Leading the 4th-highest card in a suit when a player lacks a sequence. This allows partner to apply the Rule of 11. Applies more often in notrump than in suit contracts.

Go to Bed With – Failure to take an obvious winner.

Grab – Too many players are anxious to win tricks as soon as they can, without considering the big picture. Good players don't grab tricks; they develop them.

Holding – The cards one is dealt in a particular suit.

Hold-Up Play – Refusing to immediately win a trick in the hopes of cutting the opponents' communication.

Inference – A conclusion drawn from an action by either partner or the opponents.

Intermediates – Tens and nines (and even eights). Good players appreciate these cards, while less-experienced ones often do not.

Interior Sequence – Consecutive cards within a suit where the top card is not part of the sequence; for example K J 10 9. The J 10 9 is the interior sequence. The correct lead is the jack, the top of the sequence.

"Last is Best" – A Bergenism that emphasizes the huge advantage enjoyed by the defender who plays fourth when a suit is led.

Left Heft – Slang for leading a suit when the hand to your left contains strength. See *through strength.*

Merrimac Coup – The deliberate sacrifice of a high card to knock out a vital entry to an opponent's hand, usually the dummy.

MUD – (stands for middle, up, down)
A lead convention in which the original lead from small cards is the middle card. The defender will follow with a higher card to deny a doubleton.

Neutral Lead – A passive lead that neither threatens to develop tricks nor risks the loss of tricks.

Odd-Even Discards (Roman Discards) – Used only when each defender is making his first discard. An odd-numbered card is encouraging, while an even-numbered card is discouraging and expresses suit-preference.

Overruff – Overtrumping an opponent.

Overtake – The play of a higher card than the one partner played in order to unblock or to win the trick in your own hand.

Parity – A defender would like to preserve the same length in a suit as is held by the declarer or dummy. This is most relevant with a 4-card suit.

Passive Defense – Avoiding risky leads that might give declarer a trick he couldn't have won on his own. *Passive defense* is often the best approach.

Pitch – Slang for discard.

Present Count – When declarer leads a suit that had been led previously, if possible, the defenders should still signal their count at *this* time.

Pumping Declarer – Slang for forcing declarer to ruff. See *forcing game.*

Retain the Lead – Lead a winning card, which allows you to lead to the next trick.

Return – Lead back partner's suit.

Right Light – Slang for leading a suit where RHO is weak. See *up to weakness.*

Ruff and Sluff – When a defender leads a suit in which both declarer and dummy are void, declarer can trump (ruff) in one hand and discard (sluff) a loser from the other. This is usually bad defense, but occasionally is the best move.

Rule of 11 – After partner makes a 4th-best lead, the other defender should subtract the value of the card led from 11. The difference represents the number of higher cards held by the other three players (excluding the opening leader). While this does apply in suit contracts, it is more relevant in notrump.

Run – Cash all the winners in an established suit.

Safe Lead – A lead that is unlikely to give declarer an undeserved trick. Leading 4th-best may set up tricks, but *is not safe.* Leading a weak suit *is safe,* but has limited potential. Leading the top of a 3-card sequence *is safe* and may very well be productive.

"Second Hand Low" – Playing a small card when your RHO leads a suit, because your partner still has a chance to compete for the trick. Recommended in general, but there are many, many exceptions.

Sequence – Consecutive cards in the suit, headed by at least one honor.

Set – Defeat the declarer's contract.

Set Up (Develop) (Establish) – Promote a card (or cards) into winners by forcing out the declarer's higher card(s) in that suit.

Shift – Lead a different suit than the one the partnershift led earlier in the hand.

Short Hand (Short Side) – The partnership hand that has fewer cards in the suit in question.

Show Out – Fail to follow suit.

Side Suit – Any suit other than trumps.

Signals – Plays made by the defenders to give each other information.

Spot Cards – Any card from two through nine.

Suit-Preference Signal – The one signal that is sometimes given with a lead. It is used in various situations when you want partner to lead a particular suit. A high card strongly suggests that partner lead the higher-ranking of the remaining suits;
a low card suggest the lower-ranking suit.

Surrounding Play – An advanced technique after seeing dummy's cards. A defender breaks a suit by leading his second-highest card (usually an honor) in that suit.

"Third-Hand High" – The play of a high card to try to win the trick or prevent your LHO from winning a trick cheaply. Used when competing for the trick in a suit that partner led. This is good general advice, but there are many exceptions.

Timing – The order in which suits are played. All defenders strive to learn good timing.

Through Strength – Leading a suit when the hand on your left has strength in that suit. This is not nearly as attractive as many players believe it to be.

Top of a Sequence – Leading the highest card from a holding such as Q J 10 x is a *very* desirable lead in both suit contracts and notrump.

Top of Nothing – A method of leading the highest card in a suit to deny an honor.

Touching Honors – Adjacent honors, such as the queen and jack.

Trump Control – A defender's trump holding that prevents declarer from immediately drawing trumps. Axx is ideal. The best time to look for ruffs is when you have trump control as well as a short suit.

Trump Promotion – An extra trump trick created by the defense, sometimes based on an overruff.

Unblock – Playing or discarding a high card that would otherwise have prevented partner from winning all the tricks he was entitled to in that suit.

Uppercut – Promoting a trump trick for the defense based on the potential for an overruff.

Upside-Down Signals – The opposite of standard signals. For example, in upside-down attitude, a low card encourages, and a high card discourages.

Up to Weakness – Leading a suit when the hand on your right has no strength in that suit. This is usually a worthwhile principle, but is not the money-back guarantee that many believe it to be.

"Use Up the Honor(s) From the Short Side First"– Excellent general advice to avoid blocking the suit you are leading.

xxx – A holding of any three small cards in a suit.

xxxx – A holding of any four small cards in a suit.

Yarborough – Originally, a hand with no card above a nine. These days, a hand with no card above a 10.

YBTJ (You Be The Judge) – A popular way to evaluate "where did we go wrong?" in post-mortem analysis. Initially described in *The Bridge World.*

Appendix

Odd-Even Discards:
pages 204-208

Upside-Down Signals:
pages 209-210

Improve Your Discards – Even the Odds

Standard discards serve as attitude signals: high cards are encouraging, while low cards are discouraging. Unfortunately, these methods are often inadequate. Consider the following:

1. How do you encourage with A Q 3 2?
2. How do you discourage with 10 9 8?
3. What do you do when you cannot afford to discard in the suit you want led (for example, a strong 3-card suit such as A Q J or K Q 10)?

Problems, problems! There is definitely a better way. **When a defender is making his first discard in either a suit contract or notrump:**

an odd card (3, 5, 7, 9) is encouraging;

an even card (2, 4, 6, 8, 10) is discouraging.

In addition, an even card gives suit-preference.

A *low* even card encourages the lower-ranking of the other two suits.

A *high* even card encourages the higher-ranking of the other two suits.

This proven discarding technique is known as *Odd-Even Discards* or *Roman Discards*. When you need to express your attitude on your first discard, Odd-Even Discards allow great flexibility. Most players take to them as easily as ducks to water!

Odd-Even Discards are an example of a convention involving signals. Yes, there are conventions for defense just as there are for bidding.

Practice with the following hand. You are East and your opponents bid briskly to 4♠. You try to *will* partner to lead your nice diamond suit, but he leads the ♠K.

Contract: 4♠
Lead: ♠K

North
♠ 4 3 2
♡ 8 4
◇ A J 10 9 6
♣ Q 4 3

West
♠ A K
♡ A J 3 2
◇ 8 4
♣ J 7 6 5 2

East (You)
♠ 6
♡ 10 9 7 6 5
◇ K Q 3 2
♣ 10 9 8

South
♠ Q J 10 9 8 7 5
♡ K Q
◇ 7 5
♣ A K

West	*North*	*East*	*South*
—	—	—	1♠
Pass	2♠	Pass	4♠
All Pass			

After winning his ♠K, West continues with the trump ace. With standard signals, you are not well-placed. You'd like to tell West that you love diamonds, but hate everything else. However, both of your diamond spot cards are low. You also don't have any way to discourage clubs because your lowest club is too "high." You can try to stop a heart shift by discarding your lowest heart, but because of North's pretty diamonds, partner will probably shift to clubs.

With Odd-Even Discards, you can easily encourage diamonds by discarding the ♢3, an odd-numbered card. But, also consider the ♡10. As an even card, it discourages hearts. In addition, its status as a high spot card shows your preference for diamonds, the higher-ranking of the other two suits. Isn't it nice to have this option? The ♡10 discard would be crucial if your ♢3 was an even-numbered spot; then the only way to ask for diamonds would be a high even heart.

You select the ♡10; preferring to tell partner about your holding in two suits at once. Partner looks that over, and loyally shifts to the ♢8. Because the N-S clubs are blocked, if declarer grabs the ♢A, he can't get to dummy's ♣Q to discard his diamond loser. When he plays dummy's ♢J, you win your queen and return a heart for the setting trick.

"Thanks for the great signal, partner," says West. "Without that discard, diamonds is the *last* suit I would have shifted to."

When armed with Odd-Even Discards, you can make life easy in many non-obvious situations.

Contract: 3NT
Lead: ♠Q

North
♠ 7 5 3
♡ K 3
♢ K Q 10 8 7 3
♣ K 8

West
♠ Q J 10 9
♡ 6 5 2
♢ A 6 5
♣ 9 7 3

East (You)
♠ 8 4 2
♡ 10 9 8 7
♢ 4 2
♣ A Q J 10

South
♠ A K 6
♡ A Q J 4
♢ J 9
♣ 6 5 4 2

West	*North*	*East*	*South*
—	—	—	1NT
Pass	3NT	All Pass	

If this deal looks familiar, it's because it appeared on page 23. Now you hold the East cards. Declarer wins the ♠Q lead with the king, while you contribute the deuce. He plays three rounds of diamonds until West wins his ace. On the third round, you need to find a discard that will tell partner that you're dying for a club shift.

Now that you are familiar with Odd-Even Discards, telling partner about your magnificent clubs is a breeze. On the third round of diamonds, discard the ♠4. This even card says that you don't like spades. Yes, I know that partner already knew that. But, the added significance of this discard is that because the ♠2 was played earlier, partner will easily be able to recognize it as a *low* even card.

Remember, discards of even cards also serve as suit-preference signals. Discarding a *low* even card shows strength in clubs, the lower-ranking of the two remaining suits. West will lead a club, and you'll run the suit.

No muss, no fuss – as opposed to those playing standard signals, who can do no better than discard their ♡7 and pray that West will figure out that you intend the seven to be a *low, discouraging signal.*

In fact, if your hearts and clubs were reversed, with Odd-Even Discards, you'd still have an easy answer. Now, your first discard will be the ♠8. In addition to discouraging spades, this *high* even card encourages hearts, the higher-ranking of the remaining suits.

Odd-Even Discards are superior to standard discards, and, with a little practice, prove to be easy to use. You may even decide that they are also a lot of fun. Try them – only your opponents will regret it!

Food for Thought

Here are the three categories:

1. **Upside-down attitude** – A low card is encouraging; a high card is discouraging.
2. **Upside-down count** – A low card signifies an even number of cards; a high card indicates an odd number.
3. **Upside-down suit preference** – A low card asks for the higher-ranking relevant suit; a high card asks for the lower-ranking one.

Question 1: Why do some players switch to upside-down signals?

Answer: Upside-down attitude signals are based on the very sound principle that when you're giving an encouraging signal, you'd prefer to part with a low card and hang on to all your high cards. If you are encouraging from a suit such as K Q 9 2, are you sure you can afford the nine? Wouldn't it be better if you could encourage with the two? It is if you agree to signal upside-down.

Similarly, if you want to give count from four cards, isn't it nice with 10 9 3 2 to give upside-down count with the deuce? Playing standard count, you could only show an even number by playing the 10 or 9, which could cost a trick.

Question 2: "Marty do *you* recommend switching to upside-down signals?"

Answer: If you are happy with standard signals, there's no reason to consider switching. On the other hand, you may believe that just as standard bidding is sometimes inadequate, standard signals don't always get the job done. In that case, perhaps you'd like to try one or more of the three upside-down signals.

Do keep in mind that it costs nothing to experiment. If you give upside-down signals a try but are not comfortable, you can always go back to standard.

Question 3: "You said above 'one or more of the three upside-down signals.' I was told it was all or nothing. Can you play 1 or 2 of the upside-down signals, but right-side up on the other(s)?"

Answer: Absolutely. While it seems logical to use the same approach for all three signals, almost no one uses upside-down suit preference signals. In my long-time partnership with Larry Cohen, switching to upside-down attitude signals was very comfortable for both of us. However, while we understood the advantages of upside-down count, we found that switch to be awkward. We never even considered switching to upside-down suit preference.

Highly Recommended

Future Bridge Cruises with Marty Bergen

For more information, call 1-800-367-9980.

All who take a cruise with Marty will receive a copy of a Bergen book. Groups of 5 or more who sign up together will also receive a free private lesson with him.

Hardcover Books by Marty Bergen

Bergen for the Defense	$18.95
Declarer Play the Bergen Way	$18.95
MARTY SEZ...	$17.95
MARTY SEZ... Volume 2	$17.95
MARTY SEZ... Volume 3	$17.95
POINTS SCHMOINTS!	$19.95
More POINTS SCHMOINTS!	$19.95
Schlemiel...Schlimazel? Mensch (not a bridge book)	$14.95

•• SPECIAL OFFER ••

Buy one of Marty's hardcover books from him
and receive a **free** copy of any one
of his eight most recent softcover books.
Personalized autographs available upon request.

Softcover Books by Marty Bergen

Buy 2, then get 1 (equal or lesser price) for half price

Bergen's Best Bridge Tips $7.95

Bergen's Best Bridge Quizzes, Vol. 1 $7.95

To Open or Not to Open $6.95

Better Rebidding with Bergen $7.95

Understanding 1NT Forcing $5.95

Hand Evaluation: Points, Schmoints! $7.95

Introduction to Negative Doubles $6.95

Negative Doubles $9.95

Better Bidding With Bergen –
Volume 1: Uncontested Auctions $11.95
Volume 2: Competitive Bidding $11.95

Books by Eddie Kantar

A Treasury of Bridge Tips $11.95

Take Your Tricks (Declarer Play) $12.95

Defensive Tips for Bad Card Holders $12.95

Special Discount!

365 Bridge Hands with Expert Analysis
~~$13.95~~ only $5

Interactive CDs by Marty Bergen

POINTS SCHMOINTS! ~~\$29.95~~ \$25
A play-along version of the award-winning book.

Marty Sez... ~~\$24.95~~ \$20
114 of Bergen's best bridge secrets.

Very Special Offer:
Get both CDs for \$30.

For free demos of Bergen CDs, e-mail Marty at:
mbergen@mindspring.com

Software by Mike Lawrence

(first five are now also available for Macintosh)

Counting at Bridge ~~\$34.95~~ \$30
Shows you ways to gather and use information.

Private Bridge Lessons, Vol. 1 ~~\$34.95~~ \$30
Declarer techniques that everybody needs to know.

Private Bridge Lessons, Vol. 2 ~~\$34.95~~ \$30
Over 100 hands with interactive feedback.

Defense ~~\$34.95~~ \$30
Avoid errors and take as many tricks as possible.

Two Over One ~~\$34.95~~ \$30
Many hands to maximize your game and slam bidding.

Conventions **Special sale!!** ~~\$60.00~~ **\$35**
A must for every partnership.

CDs by Larry Cohen

Play Bridge With Larry Cohen

An exciting opportunity to play question-and-answer with a 19-time national champion. "One of the best products to come along in years. Easy-to-use. Suitable for every player who wishes to improve his scores."

Day 1	~~$29.95~~	$20!
Day 2	~~$29.95~~	$20!
Day 3	~~$29.95~~	$20!

Books by Larry Cohen

To Bid or Not to Bid - The Law of Total Tricks	$12.95
Following the Law - The Total Tricks Sequel	$12.95

CDs by Kit Woolsey

Cavendish 2000:

Day 1	~~$29.95~~	$20!
Days 2-3	~~$29.95~~	$20!

Software by Fred Gitelman

Bridge Master 2000	~~$59.95~~	$48

"Best software ever created for improving your declarer play."

• • FREE SHIPPING ON ALL SOFTWARE • •
(in the U.S.) if you mention this book

The Official Encyclopedia of Bridge

(Fifth Edition – almost 900 pages)

Highlights include extensive sections on:
suit combinations, explanations of all conventions, techniques for bidding, defense, leads, declarer play, and a complete glossary of bridge terms.

The encyclopedia retails for $39.95.
Marty's price: $24 + shipping,
which inludes a free softcover book (choice of 8).

ORDERING INFORMATION

To place your order, call Marty toll-free at:

1-800-386-7432

All major credit cards are welcome.

Or send a check or money order (U.S. funds), to:

Marty Bergen
9 River Chase Terrace
Palm Beach Gardens, FL 33418-6817

Please include $3.50 (S&H) for each order.